BEYOND MONOGAMY

INTERSECTIONS

Transdisciplinary Perspectives on Genders and Sexualities

General Editors: Michael Kimmel and Suzanna Walters

Beyond Monogamy

*Polyamory and the Future
of Polyqueer Sexualities*

Mimi Schippers

NEW YORK UNIVERSITY PRESS
New York

NEW YORK UNIVERSITY PRESS
New York
www.nyupress.org

References to Internet websites (URLs) were accurate at the time of writing. Neither the author nor New York University Press is responsible for URLs that may have expired or changed since the manuscript was prepared.

ISBN: 978-1-4798-0159-6 (hardback)
ISBN: 978-1-4798-8622-7 (paperback)

For Library of Congress Cataloging-in-Publication data, please contact the Library of Congress.

New York University Press books are printed on acid-free paper, and their binding materials are chosen for strength and durability. We strive to use environmentally responsible suppliers and materials to the greatest extent possible in publishing our books.

Manufactured in the United States of America

10 9 8 7 6 5 4 3 2 1

Also available as an ebook

For Scott and Marc

CONTENTS

ACKNOWLEDGMENTS

Though the actual writing took a year, this book has been in the making for a very long time. There are so many people, too many to name specifically, who have crossed my path briefly, stayed for a bit and moved on, decided to stay, or have been there from the get-go and forever. I could not have done this without having had the experiences I've had with them all. Thank you.

I would also like to thank the many feminist, queer, and critical race theorists who have courageously blazed paths and, by doing so, made the going easier for me. My mentors throughout my education, some known and some read, in sociology, cultural studies, women's studies, gender studies, and sexuality studies—thank you. Thank you, Sociologists for Women in Society, for the work you do and for being an organization that provides mentorship and opportunity to me and to so many others.

There are also the brilliant scholars who have provided critiques and advice before, during, and after the writing. I would like to thank Laurel Westbrook and Lisa Brush for feedback on the book proposal, and Katherine Frank and Ryan Scoats for reading the chapter on threesomes and providing suggestions as well as inspiration through their own research. I thank Lisa Wade for reading the manuscript and giving me invaluable insight, advice, and encouragement. I also want to thank Michael Kimmel and his graduate students for reading part of an early draft of the book and offering lively discussion as well as critiques and suggestions.

I want to thank my students at Tulane University for inspiring me in so many ways, and those who have taken more recent classes on polyqueer sexualities for reading chapters while in process and offering critiques and encouragement. Also, thank you to my colleagues at

Tulane University, especially Michele Adams and Nancy Maveety, for providing the opportunity to teach classes with a sole focus on poly-queer sexualities.

I would like to thank my editor, Ilene Kalish, at NYU Press and the anonymous reviewers for your invaluable advice and feedback.

Thank you, Mikal Matton and Thomas Fewer, for the opportunity to bring polyamorous relationships to the counseling psychological community in New Orleans and for providing your knowledge about and insight into the psychological dynamics of polyamory.

Thank you to all of the members of the NOLA Poly Krewe for providing a safe space among like-minded folks to talk or not talk about polyamory and open relationships.

I want to especially thank Red Vaughan Tremmel for decades of friendship and long, sometimes challenging, but always safe and stimulating conversations about sex, gender, and relationships and also for giving me my first collection of erotic stories—a copy of *Herotica* signed by the editor, Susie Bright—introducing me to the wonderful world of erotic fiction.

I want to take this opportunity to thank the individuals and couples I have dated or with whom I've had the pleasure of being poly or polyish, and who shall remain anonymous. You know who you are, and I thank you for teaching me about intimacy, friendship, and love, and for helping me learn through and recover from mistakes. I also need to give a shout-out to D.M. for so much inspiration.

I would like to thank the people who have, by being friends, role models, interlocutors, and/or allies provided support, laughter, curiosity, skepticism, intellectual stimulation, opportunities, and sometimes all of the above (in no specific order): Erica Dudas, Darrin Butler, Yolanda Butler, Rachel Dangermond, Chriselda Pacheco, Marnie Beilin, Meredith Berlin, John Allen, Sarah Jane Duax, Julia Skop, Marigold Pascal, Michelle Bell, Tiyi Schippers, Rachael Davis, Kate Schippers, Pete Schippers, Jarrod Broussard, Kat Wittenburgh, Susie Bright, Danielle Hidalgo, Joseph Makholm, Kevin Lawrence Henry Jr., Christine Gladney, Vicki

Meyer, Tatjana Pavlovic, Jeff Stacey, Antoine Drye, Vernon Andrews, Elisabeth Sheff, Yvette Pettee, Vic Granata, Stephen Getman, Stephen Medina, Revati Alice Locke, Dana Berkowitz, D'Lane Compton, Andy Hendron, Lizzy Edwards Hendron, Blake Haney, Susan Woods Haney, Linda Troeller, Leah Guey, Tom McDonald, Dion Van Niekerk, Kenneth Finnegan, Vincent Marini, Scott Brothers, Jon Joslin, Jay Holtman, and Jim Coffin.

I would like to thank my home and family: my parents who, in their own way, taught me that polyamory can come in all shapes and sizes, and who have recently become surprisingly understanding of my life choices; New Orleans for being what it is, and for nurturing and challenging me, but most of all, for embracing me with its beautiful, sultry, sometimes horrific histories and cultures of non-monogamy and bawdy sexuality; and Ansel and Stevie for wresting me away from the computer, pestering me to go to the park, and encouraging me to be outside and enjoy life.

Last and mostly, I wish to thank Marc Pagani and Scott Bullock for your courage and love. Marc, you have inspired, shaped, and supported me in so many countless ways. From the mountains to the sea, to the deserts and cities, we took the world by the tail and lived a truly amazing and exciting life together. I am who I am because of you, and I will be forever grateful. Scott, I knew you long before we ever met. You see things in me that no one else does and honor me in so many ways. Your talent inspires me, your open heart humbles me, and your patience, perseverance, and strength amaze me every day. I could not have done any of this without each and both of you. Thank you.

Introduction

Polyqueer Sexualities

A man and woman are in an open relationship. They have agreed that having sexual partners outside of their couple relationship is permissible. One night, when her partner is in another city, the woman has sex with the man's best friend.

A man is in love with two people at the same time. He is under tremendous pressure from his family and community to be a respectable black man by attending church, having a successful career, and marrying a beautiful, talented, and smart black woman. The woman he loves is perfect, and he wants to marry her. However, he is also in love with his best friend, with whom he has a sexual relationship. While he loves this man and has loved other men, he has never felt at home in the "gay community" and does not identify as gay. His best friend is well aware of his relationship with the woman, but the woman has no idea he is in love with his best friend.

A woman has a twelve-year affair with a man other than her husband. Over the twelve years, despite pleas from her lover to leave her husband, she refuses because she loves them both. One evening, her husband—knowing he shouldn't, but unable to resist the temptation—listens to a voicemail message on his wife's cell phone. It is a message from her lover saying that he can't live without her and needs to see her. Enraged, the husband swears to himself that he will find the other man and kill him.

A married man tells a friend that he and his wife had a threesome with another woman. With pride, he tells the friend that it was "every guy's dream" and that he had a great time. When the friend asks him if he'd ever have a threesome with his wife and another man, he balks with repulsion and says, "No way. I'm not gay, and I would never want to see my wife have sex with someone else."

What do these vignettes have in common? With whom do you identify, if anyone? Do you judge some and sympathize with others? While most people might read these vignettes and cringe and shake their heads in disgust at the disruption and possible destruction of the heterosexual couple through sexual infidelity, I see potentialities.

Advocating for queer utopian politics, José Esteban Muñoz (2009) writes, "Unlike a possibility, a thing that simply might happen, a potentiality is a certain mode of nonbeing that is eminent, a thing that is present but not actually existing in the present tense" (9). No doubt, what is present in these scenarios is non-monogamy, and we assume that what is eminent is some kind of violation of the integrity of the couple.

We all know how these stories should unfold. A man is expected to reject the woman who becomes lovers with his best friend; choose one or the other—the perfect woman *or* a gay identity; if not kill his wife's lover, use violence to get him out of the picture; and vociferously decline the invitation for a threesome with another man. The woman, in contrast, should expect to lose her partner and her new lover—his best friend; live a "lie" because her partner is "on the down low"; end the love affair or lose her family; enjoy a threesome with another woman but never entertain the possibility of, let alone request, a threesome with another man. The only viable path is one of *either* relationship destruction and emotional trauma *or* restoring the couple through monogamy.

In her book *Queer Phenomenology: Orientations, Objects, Others*, Sara Ahmed (2007) offers a phenomenological approach to thinking about sexual orientation. According to Ahmed, heteronormativity is a "straight" line from one's position as a gendered and sexual subject to objects in the world, not just in terms of objects of desire, but also in choosing a life. She writes, "The lines we follow might . . . function as forms of 'alignment,' or as ways of being in line with others. We might say that we are orientated when we are in line. We are 'in line' when we face the direction that is already faced by others" (15). In order to be "in line" with the direction faced by others, the individuals in the vignettes above must choose monogamy. Ahmed goes on to write,

> In the case of sexual orientation, it is not simply that we have it. To be-
> come straight means that we not only have to turn toward the objects that
> are given to us by heterosexual culture, but also that we must "turn away"
> from objects that take us off this line. . . . The concept of "orientations" al-
> lows us to expose how life gets directed in some ways rather than others,
> through the very requirement that we follow what is already given to us.
> For a life to count as a good life, then it must return the debt of its life by
> taking on the direction promised as a social good, which means imagin-
> ing one's futurity in terms of reaching certain points along a life course.
> A queer life might be one that fails to make such a gesture of return. (21)

One of the objects given to us by heterosexual culture is the *monogamous couple.* In order to live a "good life" of sexual and emotional intimacy, we must turn away from other lovers. Perhaps, then, a queer life would mean reorienting oneself toward other lovers, and non-monogamy would constitute a queer life.

The people described in the situations above could "fail to make such a gesture of return" to monogamy and choose a different line. A man could accept a love affair between his partner and best friend or enthu-siastically say "yes" to a threesome with another man. What if the man who is simultaneously in love with a woman and a man were honest with himself and his lovers, refuses to identify as straight or gay, and insists on being openly polyamorous with both of them, and what if they both agree? Even the man whose wife is having a twelve-year affair could, if he chose, somehow learn to accept the "other" man as part of the family; after all, the wife and "other" man have also been in a long-term relationship and, in that sense, their relationship has been part of the family all along. What if having more than one long-term partner was available to wives as well as husbands, and tolerated or even expected across and within all races and classes?

What would have to change or be transfigured for these non-monogamous, non-dyadic outcomes to be possible? The answer, I will argue in this book, is the embodiment and structure of gendered sexuality as it intersects with race and class and manifests in individual identity, interpersonal relationships, face-to-face interactions, and cultural representations. My concern here is what *effect* poly (involving more than two people) relationship choices might have, not just on the individuals involved, but also, if chosen collectively, on social relations more generally. Discussing her own experience of entering a lesbian relationship mid-life, Ahmed writes, "Some lines might be marks of the refusal to reproduce: the lines of rebellion and resistance that gather over time to create new impressions on the skin surface or on the skin of the social" (18). What if the potentialities for polyamory become a new line or orientation? How might poly relationships and their representation "create new impressions on the skin surface" (the body and identity) or "on the skin of the social" (social structure)?

My argument is that turning away from the monogamous couple through poly sexualities offers an opportunity to reorient not just relationships, but also gender and race relations. While institutionalized and compulsory monogamy closes off the possibility of non-dyadic resolutions to the scenarios above, it is also the dominance and superiority of white heteromasculinity as a set of cultural expectations, a social location, and an embodied experience that depends on compulsory monogamy and thus obscures the queer path of poly sexualities. Stated another way, institutionalized, compulsory monogamy insists on a dyadic resolution for all regardless of gender or race, but it is gender and race privilege that are at stake in the narratives we tell about monogamy and its failures.

The central goal of this book, then, is to begin developing a theoretical framework for identifying how compulsory and institutionalized monogamy is *constitutive of and legitimates* the discursive construction and institutionalization of gender as a racialized, hierarchical binary that situates certain forms of masculinity as superior and dominant in relationship to the inferior and subordinate feminine and/or the racialized other.

I approach compulsory monogamy in a similar way to how Adrienne Rich (1983) interrogated compulsory heterosexuality. According to Rich, compulsory heterosexuality is a network or system of social beliefs, customs, and practices that compel women into intimate relationships with men. As an institution, compulsory heterosexuality systematically ensures men's access to and "ownership" of women's bodies, labor, and children. According to Rich, compulsory heterosexuality is characterized by male identification, androcentrism, and the erasure of lesbian existence, and, as such, prevents women from bonding with each other sexually, emotionally, and politically. In her groundbreaking essay, Rich suggests that woman-identification and lesbian sexuality are important to feminist practice because they refuse and disrupt compulsory heterosexuality as a central mechanism of men's dominance over and access to women.

> But whatever [compulsory heterosexuality's] origins, when we look hard and clearly at the extent and elaboration of measures designed to keep women within a male sexual purlieu, it becomes an inescapable question whether the issue we have to address as feminists is not simply "gender inequality," nor the domination of culture by males, nor mere "taboos against homosexuality," but the enforcement of heterosexuality for women as a means of assuring male right of physical, economical, and emotional access. One of the means of enforcement is, of course, the rendering invisible of the lesbian possibility, an engulfed continent that rises fragmentedly to view from time to time only to become submerged again. (191)

Like Rich, I am interested in how institutionalized sexual arrangements support heteromasculine interests and ascendancy. However, instead of focusing on the relationship between compulsory heterosexuality and patriarchal marriage, my focus is on the contemporary American context of gender and sexual politics and social relations and how the discursive conflation of the *pure relationship* (Giddens 1992) with the monogamous couple supports, legitimizes, and naturalizes a hegemonic relationship between masculinity and femininity.[1]

As a sociologist, I follow in Rich's feminist footsteps but reorient my theoretical focus away from radical feminist theory, where men are the oppressors and women are the oppressed, and toward gender sociology and queer theory to theorize the monogamous couple as central to white heteromasculine privilege and superiority and to social and cultural *regimes of normalcy* implicated in power relations and sexual stratification. I argue that consensual non-monogamy, like lesbian sexuality according to Rich, "rises . . . to view from time to time" in the feminist consciousness and feminist theory "only to become submerged again." Given the emergence in the mainstream media of polyamory as a viable relationship form, I will argue that it is imperative that feminist, queer, and critical race theorists take this opportunity to unpack mononormativity, develop an interest in the queer, feminist, and anti-racist potential of polyamory, and advocate and cultivate *polyqueer* sex and relationships.

Queer Theories of Normativity

Following Michel Foucault's claim that the proliferation of discourses of sexual normalcy is a central axis of power in modern Western cultures, queer theory interrogates the discursive construction of normal, healthy, moral desire and sexual practices not just as a mechanism of disciplinary power, but also as a contested terrain of sexual politics. Queer theorists place *normativity* at the center of understanding, interrogating, and deconstructing how institutionalized regimes of sexual normalcy are implicated in establishing and maintaining social privilege and material inequalities. As Gayle Rubin (1984) suggests, those who fall *inside* the "charmed circle" of sexual normalcy are perceived as moral and deserving citizens while those who are defined as "perverts" are cast out as social pariahs not deserving of the rights of citizenship. As a social scientist, Rubin argues that the charmed circle of sexual normalcy is not only a discursive construction; it is an organizing rationale for institutionalized structures of privilege and disadvantage. Legal definitions of family, educational goals and curricula, criminal law, and access to and protections against discrimination in employment, housing, and health care, for instance, systematically confer benefits on those who fall or are perceived to fall within the charmed circle of sexual normalcy while denying those benefits to people who do not.

In addition to focusing on patterns of sexual behavior, attitudes and beliefs about sex, and discrimination against LGBTQ populations, sociologists of sexuality also are interested in *normativity* or the workings of privilege as they play out in everyday, normative meanings and practices as well as in the policies and structure of large-scale institutions.[2] Incorporating the queer theoretical focus on regimes of normalcy, the sociological study of sexuality has expanded to include theory and research that interrogates both representations of sexuality and institutionalized practices that marginalize or erase certain erotic tastes, practices, and relationships. From a sociological perspective, our focus is on understanding how sexual normalcy is central to or an organizing rationale for social structure and social relations more generally.

Building on the work of Rich, Foucault, Rubin, and others, queer theorists and sociologists of sexuality define *heteronormativity* as the social, cultural, and institutionalized meanings and practices that systematically confer privilege in the forms of status, authority, and material resources on heterosexual people who conform to societal norms and expectations for living a "good life." Heteronormativity includes, but is not limited to, marriage between one man and one woman, a definition of family that hinges on the presence of dependent children, relationships based on love and commitment rather than sex, relationship longevity, active participation in capitalism in terms of both employment and consumption, and monogamy. As a regime of normalcy, heteronormativity privileges those who follow and embody these norms and systematically disadvantages those who do not.

More recent work in queer theory has identified *homonormativity* as the neoliberal lesbian and gay rights movements' emphasis on assimilation to heteronormativity as a strategy for gaining entrance into the charmed circle. By claiming a desire to serve in the military, legally marry, and adopt children, some lesbian and gay activists emphasize their similarity to "normal" heterosexuals as a legitimate reason for legal, social, and political citizenship. However, as many queer activists and theorists have argued, even if most gay men and lesbians gain access to the charmed circle, the regime of sexual normalcy remains intact as an institutionalized system of privilege and disadvantage. While some lesbian and gay couples—namely Western, white, middle-class, gender-conforming, and monogamous couples—clearly benefit from access to military service, marriage, and traditional family forms, those who do not look or act like "normal" (white, middle-class, gender-conforming, and monogamous) heterosexuals are still denied the rights of citizenship.

While there is no doubt that Foucault's *History of Sexuality* (1978) is a foundational text in the emergence of queer theory, he has been criticized for his glaring omission of race and racialized sexuality as major axes of power and a central structuring feature of white supremacy.[3] Siobhan B. Sommerville (2000), for instance, outlines how the emergence of sexual normalcy and definitions of "health" were contemporaneous with and inextricable from the rise of eugenic constructions of racial superiority and inferiority. The "healthy" individual was not only heterosexual; the "good citizen" was also white. Similarly, Sharon Patricia Holland (2012) points out that the notion of reproduction, central to legitimating discourses of "normal" and "healthy" sexuality and to Foucault's treatment of sexuality, is not simply about reproducing class structures, but also racial purity. Holland convincingly argues that interracial desire, sex, and relationships were as much, if not more, pathologized through discourses of "healthy sexuality" as were sexual perversions.

Foucault's omission and the dominance of white, class-privileged academics in defining the parameters of early queer theorizing led to a failure to adequately theorize white supremacy as central to regimes of sexual normalcy and black experience. For instance, E. Patrick Johnson (2001) avers that queer theory's emphasis on discourse and deconstructing identities ignores the material necessity of identity politics on the basis of race for queers of color. He suggests that, from an African American standpoint, a critical perspective on regimes of normalcy must take into consideration the racialized body.

> What, for example, are the ethical and material implications of queer theory if its project is to dismantle all notions of identity and agency? The deconstructive turn in queer theory highlights the ways in which ideology functions to oppress and to proscribe ways of knowing, but what is the utility of queer theory on the front lines, in the trenches, on the street, or anyplace where the racialized and sexualized body is beaten, starved, fired, cursed—indeed, where the body is the site of trauma? (5)

Johnson puts forward "quare theory" as a label that combines a queer theoretical analysis of regimes of sexual normalcy *and* the racialized body. Recent and provocative theoretical work by Trimiko Melancon (2014) connects representations of the racialized body with embodied erotic pleasure and power through an exploration of black women's sexuality and interracial same-gender loving.

While Sommerville, Holland, and others point to the omission of an analysis of race in queer theory, other queer of color theorists focus on the ways in which critical race theory ignores sexuality. Dwight McBride (2005), for instance, argues that notions of black respectability as a response to the exclusion of African Americans from the construction of sexual normalcy have led African American academics to remain silent about dissident sexualities and thereby erase queer sexual subjectivities from critical race theory. In an essay that originally appeared in a special issue of *Differences* on queer theory, Evelyn Hammonds (1994) is critical of the relative silence of white queer theorists on race and whiteness, but she also laments the lack of theoretical work by African American women on the ways in which race and gender shape "black queer female sexualities." In particular, Hammonds is concerned with a silence about the relationships among and between African American straight and lesbian women and queer and dissident desires and/or embodiments of African American women. She suggests that a "politics of articulation" that "would build on the interrogation of what makes it possible for black women to speak and act" (136) might replace the "politics of silence" and "politics of dissemblance" that arose within the context of the politics of respectability.

The Missing Critique of Mononormativity

In most queer and queer of color theory, monogamy is identified as a central feature of sexual normalcy in terms of heteronormativity, homonormativity, and the politics of respectability. However, there have been very few theoretical interrogations of how monogamy is implicated in and productive of gender, race, and sexual hierarchies or the role of monogamy as an organizing rationale for regimes of normalcy and social structures of inequality.[4]

Some feminist theorists have placed a more systematic analytic focus on the gender politics of heterosexual monogamy. Explaining why women do not see themselves as a coherent group with shared political interests, for instance, Simone de Beauvoir (1949) writes, "Male and female stand opposed within a primordial *Mitsein*, and woman has not broken it. The couple is a fundamental unity with its two halves riveted together, and the cleavage of society along the line of sex is impossible" (29). According to de Beauvoir, women are "riveted" to men in the "primordial" couple. Women's alliances and emotional investments are with individual men and this compromises their ability to see men as their political adversaries. As described earlier, Adrienne Rich made a similar argument, but rather than naturalize the heterosexual couple as inevitable and grounded in nature, Rich suggested that the *idea* of the "primordial couple" is a male-dominant social construction.

While Beauvoir and Rich focus on heterosexual coupling, Victoria Robinson (1997) places her focus on heterosexual *monogamy* as an institutionalized form of social control that reflects and naturalizes a capitalist and patriarchal property relationship where men possess women. Romantic monogamy encourages a woman to overinvest her energy, time, and resources into an individual man. Instead of dismissing heterosexuality as inherently male dominant, Robinson suggests that power relations within heterosexual relationships might be transformed through non-monogamy.

In a more recent article, Stevi Jackson and Sue Scott (2004) revisit the feminist argument that being in monogamous relationships with men limits women's autonomy and political consciousness. They assert that the effects of monogamy on women's lives are still important and relevant to feminists despite the disappearance of the critique of monogamy from feminist theory in recent decades.

While I agree with Jackson and Scott's assessment of how monogamy can be disadvantageous to women in heterosexual relationships, my focus in this book is less on the effects of monogamy on women's lived experience in monogamous relationships with men and, instead, more on theorizing monogamy as an institutionalized feature of social structure. Going back to Robinson's focus on institutionalized monogamy, I focus on mononormativity as a central feature of contemporary regimes of sexual normalcy. Many feminists have discussed how the practice of monogamy maintains women's subordination to men, but few have talked about the cultural and social role of the monogamous couple, as an idealized and institutionalized structure for relationships and sexual relations, in defining, maintaining, and legitimating hierarchical relationships between and among racialized masculinities and femininities.

My goal in this book is to build upon and integrate the queer, feminist, and critical race theory discussed above to develop a theoretical framework for identifying how institutionalized monogamy is, in a contemporary U.S. context, constitutive of the discursive construction and social institutionalization of gender and race hierarchies.

As one step in theorizing the intersections of monogamy, gender, and race, I will argue that monogamy is the first and largely unquestionable discourse in narratives of relationship normalcy, health, and morality and that the pathologization of non-monogamy and erasure of consensual non-monogamies situates the monogamous couple as normal, moral, and compulsory. While Adrienne Rich's emphasis was on the erasure of lesbian existence and the political potential for the lesbian continuum, I argue that the invisibility, erasure, and recent normalization of consensual non-monogamies foreclose the possibility for what I'm calling polyqueer sexualities to undo and reorganize the structure of relationships, erotic interactions, and the gendered self.

Mononormativity, Compulsory Monogamy, and Research on Consensual Non-Monogamies

Skepticism about and critiques of monogamy are not new. Since the mid-nineteenth century, there have been several experimental and/or utopian communities that adopted non-monogamy as a central tenet of communal living (DeMaria 1978; Kern 1981; Muncy 1973). In addition, research suggests that non-monogamy is common, if not culturally normative, in many gay men's relationships (Adam 2006; Bell and Weinberg 1978; Blasband and Peplau 1985; Blumstein and Schwartz 1983; Coelho 2011; Kurdek and Schmitt 1985; McWhirter and Mattison 1984; Peplau and Cochran 1981). More recently, a popular (Anapol 2004; Anapol 2010; Block 2008; Easton and Hardy 2009; Taormino 2008) and academic (Barker and Langdridge 2010a; Barker and Langdridge 2010b; Sheff 2005; Sheff 2006; Sheff 2011; Sheff 2013) literature on non-monogamies, especially open relationships and polyamory, has emerged.

Within this growing literature, researchers and activists build on the concept of compulsory heterosexuality to identify *compulsory monogamy* as the institutionalized arrangements that compel or force people into monogamous, dyadic relationships (Mint 2004). For example, laws against polygamy make monogamous coupling compulsory. The discursive conflation of monogamy with a "real" or "serious" relationship and finding "the one and only" as the brass ring of relationship satisfaction situate monogamy as romantic (Barker 2013; Robinson 1997), psychologically healthy and satisfying (Conley et al. 2013), and something worth "working" for and toward (Kipnis 2003).

For most people, there is an assumption that their relationships are or will eventually become monogamous without ever having a discussion with prospective or existing partners about monogamy. If there is a discussion, it is not about whether or not a polyamorous or open relationship is desired, but rather whether or not to forego other lovers and be monogamous as a step toward being more committed.

The idea that "hook up" culture is a phase from which young people mature and that all adults eventually "settle down" into "real" relationships dismisses non-monogamy as immature and transitional. Wedding invitations that include "plus one," limits of only two adults in a hotel room, and Valentine's Day specials that are two-for-one reflect the assumption that the couple is the only legitimate and intelligible form for intimate relationships.

Even more pernicious are the many rules, regulations, laws, and policies that assume dyadic relationships and render polyamorous relationships, where individuals have intimate and committed relationships with more than one person, unintelligible. Laws prohibiting polygamy have huge consequences in terms of child custody, insurance, participation in health care decisions, hospital or prison visitation, inheritance, and so on. There are no laws that prohibit housing or employment discrimination on the basis of relationship status, and so people in polyamorous families or relationships are at risk of both.

Compulsory monogamy also renders consensual non-monogamies perverse, impossible, or a threat to "normal" relationships. For instance, family and friends of polyamorous people often fail to recognize more than one partner, or they perceive or treat new partners as threats to existing relationship(s) (Barker 2005; Mint 2004). In contrast to the social accolades and support that come with coupling in a monogamous relationship, often times others will push back with warnings about how such a relationship could never work. The resulting lack of social recognition and support puts a tremendous strain on polyamorous relationships.

Because people in polyamorous relationships are falsely assumed to be promiscuous and always looking for new partners, we are sometimes rejected by monogamous friends out of fear we will pursue their partners and destroy their relationships. Many monogamous couples will socialize only with other monogamous couples as a way to eliminate temptation (Frank and DeLamater 2010). People in poly relationships are often assumed to lack respect for monogamy and to be willing to cross the boundaries made by others. All of these examples not only push people into forming monogamous couple relationships, they also privilege those who "succeed" in doing so.

Like the queer theoretical concept heteronormativity, these are examples of *mononormativity*, which refers to the institutionalized arrangements and cultural narratives that situate the monogamous dyad as the only legitimate, natural, or desirable relationship form, thereby systematically conferring privileges on those who are or appear to be in monogamous couples (Pieper and Bauer 2005) and disadvantages on those who are not, whether single or poly. In Pieper and Bauer's and others' discussions of mononormativity, the emphasis is not on sexual identities or practices, but instead on *relationship form* as variable and central to the operations of sexual stratification in contemporary U.S. and European contexts.

Though mononormativity intersects with heteronormativity, institutionalized dyadic monogamy confers privileges and advantages on people in or perceived to be in long-term, monogamous couple relationships regardless of the race, gender, or sexual identities of the partners. In other words, mononormativity is part of the regime of sexual normalcy, but it is not the same thing as heteronormativity. Mononormativity operates through its own logic of privileging monogamy, not heterosexuality. Despite being disadvantaged by heteronormativity, monogamous gay and lesbian couples benefit from mononormativity. Similarly, the politics of respectability are structured not just by heteronormativity, but also mononormativity. Clearly, white heterosexual couples reap far more material, social, and cultural benefits than heterosexual African American or gay or lesbian couples by being monogamous and coupled, as has been documented by decades of social science research. The point here is not to dispute or supplant heteronormativity with mononormativity, but instead to add mononormativity to feminist and queer critiques and analysis by highlighting how being in a long-term, monogamous couple relationship gets one closer to being "normal." Moreover, and more central to my purposes here, as is the case with heteronormativity, the monogamous dyad, as an institutionalized and compulsory relationship form, not only privileges the monogamous couple, it also intersects with race and gender to support white supremacy and heteromasculine dominance.

Polyamory as an Emerging Relationship Form and Culture

"Polyamory" refers to committed, emotionally and sometimes sexually intimate relationships involving more than two persons. Polyamory is often distinguishable from "cheating" in that, unlike in monogamous relationships where one partner covertly has sex with someone else, in polyamorous relationships all partners are aware of each other and consent to the relationship (Anapol 2004; Easton and Hardy 2009; Mint 2004; Taormino 2008).

Moreover, polyamory is not the same thing as male-dominant forms of polygamy in that there is an emphasis on and expectation of gender egalitarianism (Cascais and Cardoso 2012; Easton and Hardy 2009; Sheff 2013; Taormino 2008). Unlike polygyny, where one man has more than one wife but women are limited to one husband, in polyamory, access to multiple partners is acceptable for all genders. Rather than creating a shortage of women, which in the context of polygyny often increases competition and hierarchies among men and exacerbates inequality among men and between men and women, polyamory expands the number of available partners to all adults. (For a critique of the comparison between polygyny and polyamory, see Rambukkana 2015.) As a result, those who are already attached are, in theory, available to others as potential partners. In fact, because of its emphasis on gender egalitarianism and because there is no limit to the number of partners any individual might have, polyamory decreases the competition borne of scarcity that is found in monogamy as well.[5]

While polyamory increases available partners in terms of numbers and is therefore quite different from polygyny and monogamy, there are other aspects of polyamory as a subculture that mitigate competition and bolster gender egalitarianism (Cascais and Cardoso 2012). Until recently, polyamory as a viable relationship option has remained outside mainstream culture. Because of its marginalization, a relatively coherent subculture of collective understandings and behavioral ethics has emerged among polyamorists through online blogs and forums, how-to books, podcasts, and localized community organizing. Ritchie and Barker (2006) demonstrate how mononormativity necessitates development of a new language and how new discourses about emotional and sexual intimacy change the experience of intimate relationships for polyamorists.

For instance, polyamorists offer alternative languages and collective understandings of sexual jealousy. "Compersion" in the American and "frubbly" in the British context are words used by polyamorists to refer to feeling pleasure (rather than fear or anger) when one's partner experiences pleasure with another person. Because poly subcultural norms insist upon gender egalitarianism, everyone, regardless of gender, is encouraged to cultivate compersion rather than jealousy and to feel frubbly rather than frightened or angry when a partner is emotionally or sexually involved with another person. Not only is this a counternarrative to the evolutionary anthropological assumption that sexual jealousy is "natural" or biologically intrinsic among men (more on this in the next chapter), it also encourages women to reject the idea that other women are competitors for men's attention.

Redefining the structure of relationships also encourages cooperation rather than competition among men and women. So, for instance, another relationship innovation to mitigate jealousy and competition is a subcultural expectation for open communication and an ethic of care, not only for one's partner(s), but also and significantly, one's partner's partners, a role polyamorists call "metamour." For example, two men who are in an intimate and committed relationship with the same woman would be considered metamours. The label not only situates a partner's partner as a recognizable and legitimate social location in intimate relationships, it also establishes interpersonal expectations and responsibilities between metamours. There are strong expectations that metamours will develop lines of communication, and in some cases, emotional ties with each other.

As I will explore further in this book, this has important implications for gender relations and racialized masculinities, femininities, and the relationships among and between them. Moreover, because emotional intimacy and interpersonal responsibility among and between more than two people is the defining feature that distinguishes polyamory from monogamy and sexually open relationships,[6] it can be productive of feminist and queer potentialities that would not otherwise arise within the context of polygyny or monogamy (Wilkinson 2010).

Empirical research on people who have open relationships and/or participate in swinging and/or polyamory consistently shows that gendered power dynamics are affected by consensual non-monogamies in ways that disrupt or undermine male-dominant understandings and workings of gendered sexuality (Sheff 2005; Sheff 2006; Frank 2008; Frank 2013). However, we still do not have a theoretical framework with which to *explain* the effects of consensual non-monogamies on gender and power.

Empirical work on open and polyamorous relationships also consistently finds that the people who identify as polyamorous and/or who participate in activism or community building around poly identities or practices are overwhelmingly white and middle class (Sheff 2014). Christian Klesse (2014) links polyamory subcultures to capitalism and neoliberal cultural politics to begin unpacking the class homogeneity of polyamorous communities and activists. However, while most researchers acknowledge that the racial homogeneity of research participants is an issue of methodology (snowball sampling, racial homogeneity of researchers, different definitions of "community," etc.) and not necessarily a reflection of the racial identities of people practicing some form of consensual poly sexualities, most of this empirical work lacks a theoretical framework that can explain why people who identify as open or poly and their communities and organizations are overwhelmingly white.

Polynormativity

Polyamory, like other forms of intimate and sexual relationships, is a result of and embedded within patterns of significant social change, but is also mired in contemporary social circumstances. Included in those social circumstances are persistent gender and racial inequality and an emphasis on neoliberal solutions for social and cultural problems. For this reason, there is a small critical voice in the blogosphere and in academia raising concerns about *polynormativity*. Polynormativity refers to beliefs, practices, and values within polyamory that reflect and sustain regimes of sexual and relationship normalcy and/or social privilege along the lines of class, race, gender, religion, citizenship, and so on. As blogger Sex Geek writes in an entry entitled "The Problem with

Polynormativity" (Zanin 2013), "The problem—and it's hardly surprising—is that the form of poly that's getting by far the most airtime is the one that's as similar to traditional monogamy as possible, because that's the least threatening to the dominant social order."

For instance, in the wake of the marriage equality movement, some polyamorists and much of the mainstream commentators on polyamory wonder if polyamory is "the new gay" in terms of marriage rights. In most cases, this is couched in speculation about whether or not polyamorists will organize around a collective movement for the legalization of plural marriage.[7] While this is an important question in terms of discrimination on the basis of relationship status, it erases important differences between being gay and/or transgender and being polyamorous. As Pepper Mint (2007) writes on his blog *Freaksexual*, "Poly people do not get queer-bashed, or anything close to it; polyamory does not induce the same level of straight-out revulsion and violent response that is engendered by violations of gender or sexuality." Moreover, polyamory does little to question legal marriage as a system of privilege and inequality (Rambukkana 2015).

Similarly, many polyamorists rely on narratives of "normalcy" to make polyamory intelligible and acceptable. To take one example, Cunning Minx, a leading poly educator and creator of the popular podcast *Polyamory Weekly*, offers advice to poly and poly curious people about specific issues or problems that are common or relevant to polyamorists. One of the tropes Minx uses on the podcast is "WWMD," as in "What would monogamists do?" This is a very effective way to situate polyamory in the continuum of relationships, and for monogamous listeners, it can make polyamory seem less foreign. While I applaud this strategy of normalization, I am less enthusiastic about the way in which it situates monogamy in the center and polyamory as "just like" or similar enough to monogamy to be intelligible.

This strategy of normalizing polyamory is strikingly similar to claims made by gay and lesbian activists that gay and lesbian families are no different from heterosexual ones and therefore deserving of the privileges of legal family status. As queer activists, critics, and theorists have argued, this constitutes a heteronormative strategy and a move away from a critique and toward an endorsement of heterosexual marriage. While it might be true that there are many similarities between monogamous and polyamorous relationships, I worry that the tendency to think through dilemmas, problems, or ethical concerns within polyamory by invoking "WWMD" closes off the possibility to hold a queer, feminist, and anti-racist critical distance from the monogamous couple as an ideal standard and as implicated in broader relations of inequality.

Eleanor Wilkinson (2010) has similar concerns and argues that polyamory can offer a new way of relating that challenges heteronormativity, but not unless polyamorists emphasize their differences rather than their similarities to white, class-privileged heteronormativity. As Wilkinson suggests, by emphasizing the similarities between monogamous and poly relationships, we run the risk of rendering invisible *poly difference* and how those differences not only challenge the hegemony of monogamous marriage as a system of benefits and privileges, but also how poly difference might offer new and effective ways to do family, kindships, and sexualities differently.

Blogger Polysingleish is also critical of emphasizing normalcy and similarities to monogamy and, while she sees the benefits of polynormativity in making polyamory acceptable as it is introduced in mainstream media, she thinks it is time for something else. She writes in an entry called "Polynormativity and the New Paradigm" (Mariposa 2013), "Polynormative [*sic*] has done much to bring poly and non monogamy into the arena of public awareness and discussion. And, it will probably continue to do so. I do believe it is now time to add poly-alternative to the mix. There are *so many ways* to be non monogamous, and there are *so* many ways to do so ethically. So many ways to be polyamorous with multiple emotional and sexual loving relationships in our lives!"

In addition to emphasizing how normal polyamory is, the mainstream media and many polyamorists consistently present polyamory and open relationships as "not for everyone," but a possible "choice" for some individuals and couples. While this challenges compulsory monogamy, it does little to elucidate the structural features of an individual's life that might constrain or enable making this "choice" (Klesse 2014; Rambukkana 2015). In his discussion of "intimate privilege," Nathan Rambukkana (2010, 2015) points to the significant role social location, including but not limited to race, class, religion, and citizenship, plays in constraining or facilitating access to transgressive relationship forms including polyamory. Similarly, in her review of the how-to poly literature, Melita Noël (2006) writes,

> The limited amount of available texts written about polyamory offer an individually-based challenge to monogamy without closely examining systemic privileges and benefits, particularly around such issues as: nationality, race/ethnicity, education, class, language, ability, age, gender, and sexuality. The possibility for meaningful challenge to and systemic change around heteronormative monogamy is limited by this pervasive focus on individual choice and personal agency. The texts reveal that polyamorists also offer a short-sighted, isolationist alternative that serves to further solidify privileges for a few rather than realize an improved reality for many. (604)

Many people offering advice to those who are in polyamorous relationships cast the pitfalls and difficulties of polyamory as resulting from interpersonal dynamics rather than social constraints and emphasize hard work and interpersonal communication rather than a restructuring of broader gender and/or race relations to remedy problems. In discussions of jealousy, for example, most advice focuses on examining one's own biography to identify emotional and psychological insecurities and working through those feelings in order to cultivate frubbly feelings of compersion. Although there is no gender structure to this encouragement—everyone, regardless of gender, is encouraged to take personal responsibility for their own feelings of jealousy and cultivate compersion—with only a few exceptions (e.g., see Veaux and Rickert

2014) there is little, if any discussion of masculinity, femininity, or the gender dynamics and structures of possessiveness and control.

Nathan Rambukkana (2015) is particularly concerned with polyamorists' emphasis on consent and communication rather than internal power dynamics.

> Since forms of power and privilege have affects across different realms of personal and social interaction, honesty (although extremely important) does not on its own flatten out those relationships, and a polyamory that does not take this into account often does little to address those unfair relationships and can instead conceal their unfairness under the banner of being open and, *consequently*, equal. (120; italics in original)

Janani Balasubramanian (2013) writes in an entry entitled "9 Strategies for Non-Oppressive Polyamory" on the website Black Girl Dangerous,

> Polyamory doesn't get a free pass at being radical without an analysis of power in our interactions. It doesn't stop with being open and communicative with multiple friends, partners, lovers, etc. We've got to situate those relationships in broader systems of domination, and recognize ways that dating and engaging people (multiple or not) can do harm within those systems. Our intimate politics are often the mostly deeply seated; it's hard work to do.

Without a critical social analysis of the inner workings of power and privilege within polyamorous relationships, most how-to books on polyamory discuss sexism, but rarely as a dynamic *within* polyamorous relationships.

For instance, when providing advice about how to deal with mononormativity, many authors, podcasters, and bloggers will discuss the double standard and how women might face more stigma for having multiple partners (Easton and Hardy 2009; Veaux and Rickert 2014), but few discuss masculinity and the pressures on men to feel jealous, perceive other men as rivals, and police their partners' relationships with others. Elisabeth Sheff's (2005, 2006) research on gender in polyamorous relationships suggests that some polyamorous men exhibit what she calls poly-hegemonic masculinity, including "the alpha male syndrome." While most men she interviewed spoke of gender egalitarianism, some articulated the male-dominant idea that "having" many women signifies status and power while, at the same time, they relied on evolutionary excuses for having difficulty with and/or not tolerating the presence of other men in their relationships.

Sheff's (2006) research also shows that, despite an ideology of gender egalitarianism, women in poly relationships take on the majority of emotional labor. To the extent that poly relationships often require more time management and communication than monogamous ones, and emotional work is "women's work," when women are partnered with men, polyamory increases their labor. Moreover, when there are multiple women in a household, poly men face even less pressure to do their "fair share" than in monogamous relationships (Sheff 2013). These issues of gender inequity and power often get glossed over by bloggers, podcasters, and authors of how-to books.

Finally, if there is too little discussion among podcasters and how-to authors of the internal workings of masculinities, femininities, and power in polyamorous relationships and subcultures, there is also relative silence about how race, ethnicity, religion, or class shape the experience of compersion, metamour relationships, or polyamory more generally. In response, polyamorists of color are creating their own networks in local poly communities and in social media. For instance, there is a Poly People of Color (n.d.) Tumblr page and a Meetup group in New York that is specifically for black polyamorists (Black & Poly n.d.). However, most of the poly-related material in print and on the Internet pays too little attention to race and racism.

That is not to say that polyamorists are more sexist or racist than monogamists. Instead, it is to say that the mainstream and subcultural discourses about polyamory lack a sociological lens that can clarify the sexism and racism that is there. A quick perusal of the subject indices of the most popular how-to books on polyamory reveals that *none* list "gender," "race," "sexism," or "racism" as relevant topics. As the mainstream media increasingly focuses on open and polyamorous relationships as a solution to the monotony of monogamy and polyamorists continue to focus on individual strategies and ethics, we risk losing an opportunity to cultivate poly sexualities that reconfigure rather than reinscribe hegemonic notions of family, kinship, and relationships.

Nathan Rambukkana (2015) argues that heteronormative polyamory is, for the most part, a homogeneous enclave that includes very privileged people who isolate themselves and alienate others. In contrast, queer polyamory, he suggests, could be a transgressive heterotopia that articulates critical opposition to "straight" relationships and consciously works to cultivate queer spaces for relating in ways that disrupt or dismantle oppressive structures of privilege and power.

Although this scholarly and activist work on polynormativity has documented the race and class homogeneity of people who identify themselves to researchers as open or poly, and recognizes polynormativity and the need for a queer polyamory, there is not yet a coherent and comprehensive theoretical framework for linking compulsory monogamy and mononormativity to *the intersection* of gender *and* racial inequality.[8] More important, there is little in the way of articulating what a queer polyamory would look like.

To summarize then, research on polyamory provides empirical insight into some of the workings of gender, race, and class in non-monogamous relationships but lacks a coherent theory of compulsory monogamy and its constitutive role in establishing and legitimating white, heteromasculine privilege. On the other hand, feminist theory and queer theory have well-developed theoretical frameworks for the workings of heterosexism, racism, and sexism but lack a conceptual apparatus for identifying the role of compulsory monogamy and mononormativity in ensuring hegemonic gender and sexual relations as they intersect with race. It is time for research on polyamory to develop a coherent theoretical framework for the role of monogamy in social and cultural relations of inequality and for feminist, queer, and critical race theories to bring monogamy from the margins to the center of the politics of normalcy.

Toward a Sociological Theory of Mononormativity and Polyqueer Sexualities

This book brings together these two areas of research and theory—empirical work on polyamory on the one hand and feminist, queer, and critical race theory on the other—to begin filling this theoretical gap in our understanding of the role of monogamy in legitimating and perpetuating relations of social and cultural inequality. My two central theoretical goals in the book, then, are to (1) begin unpacking the links between compulsory and institutionalized monogamy and heteromasculine privilege and dominance as it intersects with race and sexuality, and (2) develop a theoretical framework for identifying and cultivating what I am calling *polyqueer sexualities*—sexual and relationship intimacies that include more than two people and that, *through plurality*, open up possibilities to "undo" race and gender hierarchies in ways that would not otherwise arise within the context of dyadic sex or monogamy.

To be clear, I am not suggesting that mononormativity or compulsory monogamy are the only or most important structuring features of race, gender, and sexual domination. Nor am I naively suggesting that polyamory will eliminate gender, race, and sexual inequalities. I do not believe that poly sexualities are "liberating" or always already feminist, queer, or anti-racist, or that monogamous relationships are, by definition, oppressive or reproductive of race, gender, and sexual inequality. Instead, I hope to convince readers that mononormativity and compulsory monogamy, as institutionalized regimes of relationship normalcy, are embedded within and constitutive of broader race, gender, and sexual regimes of domination, but through their own logic and separate from race, gender, and sexuality, obscure, legitimate, and support contemporary power relations.

In other words, they matter and, despite being a perhaps small but significant part of larger systems of social inequality and injustice, they have been largely ignored by sociologists, feminists, critical race theorists, and queer theorists. I also hope to convincingly argue that, given the role of compulsory monogamy in legitimating and perpetuating race, gender, and sexual inequalities, polyqueer challenges to mononormativity can, if done collectively, undo at least part of those systems of domination within the context of intimate relationships both in terms of their symbolic meaning and their embodied practice.

In her book *Bisexuality and the Eroticism of Everyday Life*, Marjorie Garber (2000) introduces bisexuality as the third element in heterosexual and homosexual desire. Adopting a psychoanalytic theoretical framework, Garber begins from the assumption that all desire is essentially bisexual in that it includes the psychosexual drama of children's negotiation of their relationships with mother and father. In order to secure the notion of stable homosexual and heterosexual identities, bisexuality must be suppressed and cast out of the heteronormative and homonormative charmed circles of sexual normalcy.

> [I]ssues raised by therapists, journalists, and bisexuals themselves in analyzing the ambivalent position of bisexuality in today's cultural scene are *nonmonogamy* (less supportively called promiscuity, flightiness, or instability); *maturity and immaturity* (heterosexuals often see bisexuality as a "stage" rather than an achieved condition or lifestyle; gays likewise sometimes scorn bisexuality as a "stage in the coming-out process of people who are "really" lesbian or gay); *trendiness*; and "*heterosexual privilege.*" (28; italics in original)

Though discursively denied as a viable "place" in sexual identities, bisexuality or the desire for a third element is ever present in what appears to be dyadic erotic desire and relations. Building on the work of René Girard (1965), Eve Sedgwick (1985), and Terry Castle (1993), Garber suggests that the erotic triangle is a central feature of Western narratives of the erotic couple.

> All three of these readers of Western literature—Girard, Sedgwick, and Castle—presume that what they are explaining is the erotic couple. Girard explains romantic love as triangular desire; Sedgwick sees the relations between the male rivals as the point of a structure in which they seem to compete for a woman; Castle sees relations between women as what Sedgwick and Girard leave out and what she wants to celebrate by eliminating the male mediator. . . . But what do all three analyses of coupling instate as *constitutive* of the dynamics of their pairs? Triangularity. In other words, bisexuality. In all three cases, it is bisexual triangularity that provokes, explains, and encompasses both heterosexuality and homosexuality. While all three analysts appear to privilege the couple, they all prove only that the shortest distance between two points is a triangle. (428)

As the third element in all desire and erotic coupling, Garber argues that there is a queer potential for bisexuality to unravel the notion of fixed gender and sexual identities as a reflection of unidirectional desire.

Building on this notion, I want to suggest that another and constitutive third element is non-monogamy. In Girard's, Sedgwick's, and Castle's reading of the couple, a heterosexual, homosocial, or lesbian resolution of triangularity depends on a mononormative, dyadic outcome. For Garber, bisexuality drives the triangulation of desire and she offers a treasure trove of examples from literature and popular culture to illustrate her theoretical point. Acknowledging and building on the notion that bisexuality is ever present and drives triangulated desire, here I am interested in sociologically exploring how poly sexualities are an ever-present potentiality in the social and cultural sexual field (Green 2008b) and suppressed through mononormativity to eliminate the potential for polyamory to reconfigure hegemonic gender and race relations. The third element in my exploration, then, is not bisexuality, but instead polyamory.

A Note about Methodology

In this book, I argue that The Monogamous Couple,[9] as a discursively constructed, institutionalized, and compulsory relationship form, is central to the production, maintenance, and legitimization of hetero-masculine domination and white privilege. I ask, what are the ways in which the discursive construction of The Monogamous Couple relies upon and supports race hierarchies and racialized constructions of masculinities and femininities? What happens to heteromasculinity—its dominance and superiority—when sex and relationships include more than two people?

To begin answering these questions, I bring together sociology, cultural studies, feminist theory, critical race theory, and queer theory. I also rely upon the growing empirical literature on polyamory as well as auto-ethnographic descriptions of the workings of compulsory monogamy, mononormativity, and polyqueer sexualities in my own life as a queer, feminist, white, cisgender, class-privileged, and polyamorous woman.

In addition, I adopt deconstructionist methods to discursively analyze fictional representations of polyqueer sexualities and, in some places, offer fictional narratives and fantasies of polyqueer potentialities of what could be. As a polyqueer scholar, I refuse to commit myself to one and only one theory or methodology, and as is the case with polyamorous relationships, each perspective, theory, and method brings something unique and essential to the table. In other words, while my theoretical framework is decidedly sociological, my methods are *polyqueer*.

As part of adopting a polyqueer methodology, I also incorporate multiple genres of writing. My focus in the book is to develop theory to explain and elucidate the connections between monogamy, gender, and race, but also to explore the feminist and queer potential of poly sexualities and relationships. To do so, I offer fictional narrative to both illustrate and guide readers toward an imagined polyqueer futurity. Following in the footsteps of many scholars who "queer" genre, like Gloria Anzaldua, who weaves together poetry and academic language, and Robert Reid-Pharr (2001) and John Giorno (1994), who braid sexually explicit, detailed, and autobiographical descriptions of their sexual experiences with men into their writing to theorize the political, here I include sometimes explicit descriptions of my own sexual experiences and embed short fictional vignettes about polyqueer sexual interactions and intimate relationships into my otherwise academic writing.

I build my theoretical framework through explicit descriptions of sex for two reasons. First, as a queer feminist (or feminist queer) committed to reconfiguring the social organization of sexuality, including sex negativity, I am motivated to collapse the binary between the profane pornographic and the sacred academic. Within the context of academia, the cultural construction of sex as different from and inferior to all other social phenomena leads to the marginalization of the erotic in scholarly work.[10] While sexuality and the production of sexual cultures and media products are central to the sociology of gender and sexuality, and feminist theories offer insightful and important critical elucidation of the gendered organization of sexuality, erotic and sociopolitical fantasies of doing things differently are relegated to the world of popular fiction. Catherine Waldby (1996) writes:

> Theoretical feminism is, I suspect, rather inhibited about employing an explicitly erotic or pornographic imagination because it is still for the most part caught up in the academic aesthetics and politics of reason and sobriety, and in a liberal distaste for the violence of desire. . . . [T]here are certain regrettable ways in which the absence of such an erotic imaginary leads theoretical feminism to reinscribe precisely the bodily imagos it wants to disable. If the desire to dephallicize the heterosexual male body that I have articulated here is to find further theoretical elaboration it seems crucial to draw on the resources of perversity and fantasy that can

be found both in experimental cultural work . . . and in everyday sexual practice. Maybe what theoretical feminism needs now is a strap-on. (275)

In the spirit of "strapping one on" to write feminist, queer theory, I employ "an explicitly erotic [and] pornographic imagination" to offer a peepshow, of sorts, into my own erotic experiences and *sociological* fantasies of a polyqueer futurity—a futurity that I experience as eminent in my own life and in contemporary culture.

Robert Reid-Pharr (2001) writes, "I am often asked to write about politics and culture, but I find that in most occasions the offer comes with the understanding that one will marshal the never fully stated but almost wholly appreciated modes of discretion, the deletion of pleasure, that work to keep most political writing decidedly dull and noncommittal" (10). In his refusal to do so, he says, "I offer this [explicit] image of [sex with a white lover] because I believe that in our struggle to produce an American progressivism we are lost if we discount the ways in which desire operates in the production of putatively rational decisions about government and politics. We risk the charge of hypocrisy if we offer only more and more sophisticated expressions of the anthropological gaze. We will clearly fail if we give into the fear that our dreams, our obsessions, our grubby secrets can never be vehicles for the articulation of the universal" (11). As a feminist, polyqueer sociologist, not only am I interested in documenting my "grubby secrets" so as to insert my own sexual subjectivity to theoretically penetrate heteromasculinity, I am motivated to explore what could be, both in terms of polyqueer sexualities and, as literary feminist theorists have done for at least a century, in terms of writing social critique and building sociological theory through fictional narrative.

The second reason I incorporate erotic, polyqueer narrative into an otherwise academic text is to bridge academic writing about polyqueer potentialities to polyqueer cultural production. J. Halberstam (2005) suggests that academic participants in queer culture are in a unique position to bridge the gap between academia and everyday queer cultural practice. Halberstam writes, "The queer . . . theorist and the cultural worker may also coexist in the same friendship networks, and they may function as coconspirators" (162). As an academic who is active in local poly communities and forging polyqueer relationships in my own life, I am motivated to participate in polyqueer cultural production. As Halberstam suggests, "new queer cultural studies feeds off of and back into subcultural production" (163). Here I mix polyqueer narrative with academic theorizing not only to participate in cultural production by "speaking" the language, but also to flatten the hierarchy between "low" subcultural production and "high" academic theory.

While Halberstam's focus is specifically on queer theorists' participation in queer subcultures, the idea that the marginalized academic theorist has a unique perspective and role in both academia and her community outside of academia is not new. As Patricia Hill Collins (2002) suggests in her black, feminist epistemology, the specialized knowledge of black women academics is an important conduit for the flow of ideas between academic and non-academic communities. In writing this book, one of my goals is to, from my location of situated knowledge, offer fantasy, in the form of fictional narrative, as both polyqueer cultural production and a temporary move away from the "evidence," which is always a looking back, and toward the futurity of polyqueer potentialities. This is not to say I will ignore the evidence, but that I will move beyond it through fantasies that are at once sociological and pornographic.

Finally, in this book, I specifically and exclusively explore sex and relationships that include one cisgender woman and two heterosexually identified cisgender men (WMM). While there are an infinite number of ways to do non-dyadic sex and relationships,[11] I limit my theoretical interest and analytic exploration to WMM sex and relationships because this relationship configuration, I will argue, is particularly instructive, not just in terms of the role of monogamy in hegemonic gender relations, but also in the queer and feminist potential for polyqueer sexualities and relationships to disrupt the meanings and embodiment of racialized masculinities and femininities. I am not suggesting WMM triangulation among cisgender, heterosexual women and men is the best or only non-dyadic relationship configuration for queering gender, sexuality, or mononormativity,[12] but there are several reasons it is particularly effective in *theoretically* unpacking the relationship between monogamy and hegemonic gender relations.

First, there is social and cultural tolerance for heterosexual men to have more than one woman partner (whether in the form of polygyny or in terms of the heteromasculine fantasy of having sex with two hot bisexual babes) whereas cultural narratives, social space, and/or institutionalized rituals that celebrate and condone women having more than two men partners have been, until very recently, virtually nonexistent in mainstream U.S. culture. The eroticization of WMM triangulation, like lesbian existence, has been silenced and/or erased.[13] This, I will argue, is not a coincidence. A polyamorous triad or erotic threesome between two straight-identified cisgender men and one woman is not a staple in the heterosexual imaginary precisely because it challenges heteromasculine privilege and dominance. WMM threesomes offer a cogent contrast to the hegemony of men "having" more than one woman either through polygynous marriage, a mistress, or a threesome encounter.

Another reason I limit my focus to WMM triangulation is for simplification purposes and so as to not compromise or confuse my theoretical and political argument in the minutiae of different relationship configurations. The effects of poly sexualities on gender dynamics are always going to be variable depending on the gender, age, race, class, religion, and so on of the people involved. Because there is, quite literally, an infinite number of ways to do plural relationships, it would be beyond the scope of this book to begin theorizing the gender dynamics of all configurations. That is not to say that polyqueer sexualities in gay men's and lesbian's lives and relationships are less important or theoretically insignificant; it is to say that they are beyond my scope and will, I hope, be taken up by others. While this, no doubt, will leave some readers dissatisfied and wanting more on gay, lesbian, MWW, transgender, and/or asexual poly sexualities, my hope is that this book opens up dialogue about compulsory monogamy and mononormativity so others will begin thinking about relationship form as variable and an important area of theoretical and empirical inquiry.

Finally, WMM triangulation is the analytic focus of Eve Sedgwick's foundational queer text *Between Men: English Literature and Male Homosocial Desire*. Sedgwick argues that the narrative construction of WMM triangulation as a rivalry between men for possession of the prized feminine object is a foundation for the abjection of homoerotic desire between men and central to the subordination of women. As I will argue, introducing polyamory and metamour relationships to her analysis of WMM love triangles, something Sedgwick never considered, necessitates a rethinking of homosocial desire between men and its dependence on not just the abjection of homoerotic desire, but also on compulsory monogamy.

Chapter Summaries

I started this chapter with the description of four scenarios of non-monogamy. In each chapter that follows, I will take one of those scenarios as the starting point and object of analysis to identify how *The Monogamous Couple* is implicated in racialized gender relations and heteronormativity, and to explore the polyqueer potential of poly sexualities. In chapter 1, I describe my own experience of having sex with my lover's best friend to interrogate cultural assumptions and narratives about "cheating" wives and "cuckolded" husbands. My focus will be on how the narratives we tell about infidelity reflect and sustain normative expectations for masculinity and femininity and establish The Monogamous Couple as "natural" and, in its "natural" form, restricted to white middle-class women and men.

In chapter 2, I analyze the "down low" as both a mainstream media social construction and as described by E. Lynn Harris in his novel *Invisible Life*. I will argue that the secrecy and marginalization of men on the DL reveal the centrality of monogamy in definitions of both black respectability and homonormativity. The contrast between the mainstream media construction of *The Black Man on the DL* on the one hand and Harris's personal account of secretly loving a man and a woman on the other sheds light on how dominant constructions of the DL not only perpetuate racism, heterosexism, and hegemonic notions of gender, but also mononormativity. Specifically, I demonstrate how narratives of The Black Man on the DL rely on compulsory monogamy to maintain race, gender, and sexual hierarchies and to displace anxieties about promiscuity and HIV transmission on to the bodies of young black men. Moreover, I suggest that *Invisible Life* is a polyqueer narrative of the DL in that it offers a critique of compulsory monogamy and a vision of a world in which bisexual African American men would not have to choose to be either gay or straight.

In chapter 3, I revisit Eve Sedgwick's "love triangle" as theoretically developed in *Between Men: English Literature and Male Homosocial Desire* by analyzing a contemporary fictional narrative of erotic triangulation between two men and a woman. I adopt a polyqueer lens to analyze the film *The Other Man* as a contemporary example of *polyqueer homosociality* between men. I argue that the introduction of polyamory to narratives of WMM triangulation opens space for unraveling and reconfiguring heteromasculinity in a way that disrupts the relationship between homosocial bonding and male dominance in fictional narrative and as theorized by Sedgwick.

In chapter 4, I introduce the *threesome imaginary* as a mononormative and heteromasculine fantasy of non-dyadic sexual interactions. By contrasting the heteromasculine fantasy of a threesome with two hot bi babes with a polyqueer fantasy of a WMM threesome, I will probe how erotic threesomes involving two straight men and one woman offer a phenomenological opportunity to queer the embodiment of heteromasculinity. Compulsory monogamy, I will argue, is not just about relationship form, but also translates into the normalization and strict enforcement of dyadic sex as the only legitimate kind of sexual interaction. By insisting that the only "normal" way to have sex is in pairs, compulsory monogamy fixes (1) sexual orientation as defined by the gender of the object of one's desire and (2) the phenomenological embodiment of gendered subjectivity within temporally and spatially bounded erotic interactions.

Each chapter ends with the same question from a different angle. What is the feminist, anti-racist, and/or queer potential of poly sex and relationships? José Esteban Muñoz (2009) writes, "[H]ope can be disappointed. But such disappointment needs to be risked if certain impasses are to be resisted" (9). At the risk of disappointment, I hope to shed light on mononormativity and compulsory monogamy as important, yet undertheorized regimes of normalcy that uphold hegemonic gender, race, and sexual relations, and to reorient my readers toward polyqueer sexualities as a fruitful line of feminist and queer theoretical and political intervention and innovation.

1

Man against Man

Masculinity, Femininity, and the Vilified Cheating Woman

> Maybe no one can be against love, but it's still possible to flirt
> with the idea. . . . Note that "against" is one of a few words—
> like "cleave," another—that can mean both itself and its op-
> posite. It flirts with paradox. . . . To be against means to be
> opposed: resistant or defiant. It also means next to: beside or
> near. Which leaves the problem of a phrase like "up against"
> which is indeterminate, bivalent—it can play both sides of
> the street. "Up against love": you would need to know the
> context to figure out what it means. Or alter the context—
> here's an idea to flirt with—which could make it mean some-
> thing else entirely.
> —Laura Kipnis

In this quote, from the conclusion of her polemic *Against Love*, Laura
Kipnis (2003, 201) discusses the meaning of the word "against" in the
title. The word, as Kipnis explains, is bivalent—it can mean two opposite
things, and one would need to know the context to understand which
meaning is being invoked. At the end of this quote, she suggests that
altering the context can shift the meaning of "against" to be "something
else entirely."

Like Kipnis, I am intrigued by the queerness of the word "against"—
it's bivalent meaning and its ability to "play both sides." Kipnis's polemic
is *against* monogamous love, and while I build on her work of critically
examining monogamy, I turn my attention to erotic triangulation. I will
explore how, on the one hand, the discursive construction of erotic tri-

angulation between two men and a woman situates heterosexual men *against* each other as rivals. On the other hand, as I will argue throughout the book, WMM erotic and relationship triangulation situates man *against* man in a queer closeness.

In this chapter I explore this juxtaposition by focusing on the strict taboo against a woman having sex with her partner's best friend, or to phrase it more in line with hegemonic constructions, "Bros don't poach their best friend's woman." We assume that the taboo exists because men who are intimately and sexually involved with the same woman are necessarily pitted against each other as hierarchical rivals, which is the opposite of "brotherhood." This masks the ways in which sharing a lover places men *against* each other in *queer closeness*. In this chapter I argue that the taboo does not result from the dissolution of intimacy between best friends, but instead, precludes a change in that intimacy. To make this argument, I focus on how cultural narratives about cheating husbands and wives render invisible this queer closeness between straight men by relying upon and perpetuating hegemonic constructions of and assumptions about masculinity and femininity.

Gender Difference, Sexuality, and the Monogamous Couple

Gender difference is defined and understood in contemporary Western cultures as a binary consisting of two complementary and hierarchical halves—the masculine and the feminine. The masculine and feminine are fixed as gender identities (man/woman) and what binds them together as complementary opposites is heterosexual desire—specifically, masculinity is defined as desire for the feminine object and femininity as the object of masculine desire (Butler 1990). Because subjectivity is attached to masculinity and objectification to femininity, gender difference is not just complementary; it is also hierarchical, with greater value and authority attached to the masculine. Building on Judith Butler's emphasis on the constitutive *relationality* between masculinity and femininity and R. W. Connell's (2005) definition of hegemonic masculinity, elsewhere (Schippers 2007) I developed a sociological framework for unpacking how masculinity and femininity are implicated in heteromasculine dominance and superiority. Hegemonic masculinity, I suggested, consists of "the qualities defined as manly that establish and legitimate a hierarchical and complementary relationship to femininity and that, by doing so, guarantee the dominant position of men and the subordination of women." I defined hegemonic femininity as "the characteristics defined as womanly that, when situated as inferior or subordinate in relationship to specific masculine characteristics, establish and legitimate a hierarchical and complementary relationship to hegemonic masculinity and that, by doing so, guarantee the dominant position of men and the subordination of women" (94). The key here is that gender inequality lies in and depends upon the social construction and institutionalization of the *relationship between* masculinity and femininity.[1]

The hierarchical and complementary relationship between ideals of masculinity and femininity and their relationship to each other is sociologically significant because they are an organizing rationale for social structure and social practice more generally. Assumptions about gender difference are institutionalized as the building blocks for social relations from the most micro (e.g., our sense of self, embodiment, and face-to-face interaction) to the most macro (e.g. the structure of major social institutions such as the family and global economies and political structures).

As an organizing rationale for social life, the relationship between the masculine and feminine manifests in collective beliefs about erotic and emotional interactions and attachment to define what are "normal" sex and a "good" relationship, who "belongs" together, and what the behavioral and emotional expectations are for individuals in a "good" relationship. The Monogamous Couple, as an imagined, glorified, and compulsory relationship form, mirrors and supports the discursively constructed relationship between heteromasculinity and heterofemininity.[2]

Compulsory monogamy and mononormativity, to the extent they suture one man and one woman together, support the collective assumption that The Monogamous Couple is the only "good" relationship, while also naturalizing and providing cultural legitimacy to the construction of gender difference as consisting of *two and only two* complementary and hierarchical opposites that belong together. In other words, *monogamy* as a hegemonic feature of sexual intimacy and relationships closes off the dyad as a unified and singular unit that both reflects and sustains the idea that the *gender binary* is natural and desirable.[3] Moreover, though not acknowledged in the queer of color critique of Foucault discussed in the previous chapter, compulsory monogamy precludes the possibility of cross-racial intimacies. As the only legitimate form of relationship intimacy and an articulation of the complementary relationship between masculinity and femininity *and* racial purity, the monogamous couple is heteronormative, but it is also decidedly raced and classed (Holland 2012).

Class, Race, and the Monogamous Couple

For Foucault and subsequent queer theorists, the hegemony of the monogamous couple is grounded in notions of reproduction of the heteronormative family as much as individuals. The definition of the reproductive monogamous couple as the only "healthy" and "normal" relationship form ensured the maintenance of class structures through inheritance and did so through discourses of normalcy. As discussed in the previous chapter, Sharon Patricia Holland (2012) takes this point further by emphasizing how normal desire and coupling were not only defined and produced according to gender difference and class location, but were also enforced on the basis of racial difference and sameness.

Hegemonic constructions of the monogamous couple are implicated in more than just gender inequality and heteronormativity; they are also central to colonial discourse[4] and white supremacy. If we look closely at the sociohistorical construction of the monogamous couple, it quickly becomes apparent that institutionalized policy and white-supremacist rhetoric excluded African American women and men from representations of the monogamous couple. While much has been written about controlling images of African American women as jezebels or mammies and African American men as sexual predators, here I want to emphasize the pathologization of African American families and kinship structures as incapable of marital monogamy.

During Jim Crow, for instance, images of hypersexualized African American masculinities and femininities included representations of "the acquiescence of the black husband to his wife's infidelity" (Higginbotham 1993, 190). Not only did this stereotype cast African American women as promiscuous and unfaithful to their husbands, it also emasculated African American husbands in their "acquiescence" to being cuckolded. By suturing "acquiescence to infidelity" to blackness and inferiority, marital monogamy was established as superior and attached to whiteness.

Perhaps the most pernicious example of attaching non-monogamy to blackness and monogamy to whiteness can be found in the Moynihan Report, formally titled *The Negro Family: The Case for National Action*, written in 1965 by Daniel Patrick Moynihan, then assistant secretary of labor. Moynihan's goal was to identify the causes of racial stratification in the United States. In his report, he argued that high rates of poverty and crime in African American communities resulted from a "culture" of "matriarchal" family structure. Single-parent, female-headed households with children from multiple fathers, Moynihan argued, led to the emasculation of African American men and a lack of male role models for African American boys. Moynihan's solution to poverty and crime was to establish policies that would facilitate and support male-headed, nuclear (monogamous) marriages among African Americans.

As others have argued, this blame-the-victim pathologization of African American family and kinship structures is central to institutionalized white supremacy in the United States. By situating the African American father as derelict in his duties to be a good provider, disciplinarian, and role model, all of which are central features of hegemonic masculinity as it structures the husband/father role, "good" husband/fathers have been whitened. Similarly, narratives of "matriarchal" family structures implicitly constructed African American wives/mothers as not embodying family-specific roles attached to hegemonic femininity (economic dependence on and subordination to one man, primary caretaker of husband and children).

The norm against which African Americans were compared is, of course, that of white, middle-class, suburban marriages. Moynihan's report relied heavily on juxtaposing patriarchal, monogamous marriage—framed as normal, natural, and socially desirable—against "matriarchal," non-marital, and non-monogamous relationships—framed as abnormal, unnatural, and socially maladaptive. To the extent that discourses of "multiple fathers" or "many children by multiple women" are racialized as cultural features of African American familial relations, the monogamous couple in its idealized form was discursively attached to whiteness and *mononormativity* was central to this construction.

Mononormativity, Narratives of Cheating, and Gender

Pepper Mint (2004) outlines the importance of cheating narratives in maintaining mononormativity and leaving monogamy invisible as the hegemonic norm.

> The reason we raise a common sin [cheating] to high theatre is to provide an example of what not to do. The visible reenactment of the cheating drama names a common temptation, draws a supposedly typical person into that temptation, and then lays out the terrible results of their fall from grace. The spectacle of the discovered cheater or adulterer is a modern morality play, with a fairly fixed script that is endlessly reused. In this spectacle, the cheater plays the common cultural part of the demonized other, a yardstick that normal people can measure their morals against. Like other systems of demonization, this one operates by naming the

outsider ("cheater") and leaving the normative behavior unnamed and unexamined. (58–59)

In the Durkheimian sense, the cheater is the "deviant other" against which the norm is established. As is the case with all deviance against social norms, those who violate the rules by engaging in deviance suffer social sanctions and, as they are collectively and publicly punished, others are discouraged from engaging in the behavior.

> Monogamy needs cheating in a fundamental way. In addition to serving as the demonized opposite of monogamy, the mark of the cheater is used as a threat to push individuals to conform to monogamous behavior and monogamous appearances. (Mint 2004, 59–60)

According to Mint, the ubiquity of narratives of cheating and the public spectacle of how "cheaters" suffer establish monogamy as the unstated norm while, at the same time, cheating is positioned as the inferior and immoral opposite of monogamy, as if the binary monogamy/cheating were mutually exclusive and exhaustive of the range of sexual behavior.

While Pepper Mint offers compelling, sociological conceptual linkages between narratives of cheating and mononormativity, his work does not unpack how cheating narratives are gendered and raced. The narrative we tell about cheating women is not the same as the one about cheating men, and as outlined above, non-monogamy among African Americans is narrated as something other than "cheating" and left out of the monogamy/cheating rubric of normative sexuality. Neither cheating wives nor cheating husbands are held in high social esteem and, in our narratives, all "cheaters" are deserving of severe social sanction. However, how we perceive them, interpret their behavior, and judge their character is structured by assumptions about gender and racial difference.

For instance, advice websites written by sex therapists and "infidelity experts" provide insight into just how gendered cheating narratives are.

Providing advice to both men and women with cheating spouses, the homepages of these sites send the message that infidelity is an equal opportunity experience when it comes to gender. However, virtually all of them separate explanations for *why* spouses cheat by gender.

For instance, on the Infidelity & Cheating Information Site, there are two separate links for "Why Men Cheat" and "Why Women Cheat." Clicking on these links will bring the user to pages with very different explanations for cheating. The page "The Cheating Husband" (n.d.) reads:

> Men . . . appear to be driven by the desire to feel good and to be with someone that arouses them. They often stray when they find an opportunity to have sex with someone that is "hotter" then their wife or partner or is in some way more sexually exciting. If they perceive their wife as being overweight, out of shape, non-responsive or too crabby, infidelity becomes a much more realistic option. Everyone has heard story after story about a husband who we catch cheating who reports that it is his wife's fault. "She got fat"; "she only cares about the kids" or no longer cares about having exciting sex. Men like to feel important and desired and when a woman shows an interest, it feels good and they go after it. When a stranger shows an interest in a man, they get aroused. Put a man who is unhappy at home or in his marital bed in that scenario and you can guess what happens.

For men, cheating is about arousal and feeling "good" and "important" and results from a lack of desire for their wives. They "stray" when they are unhappy. If a wife is unattractive (overweight, out of shape) or not attentive and pleasant (non-responsive, too crabby)—all, by the way, examples of a refusal to embody hegemonic femininity in relationship to husbandly hegemonic masculinity—the husband will be unhappy. An unhappy husband, it seems, is less likely to control himself when faced with an exciting "opportunity."

By contrast, the page entitled "The Cheating Wife" (n.d.) explains:

The reasons women cheat vary considerably. Some get involved in extra-marital affairs because they are lonely, others because they want to escape the monotony of marriage. Still others are motivated to cheat as a form of revenge after they find lipstick or other tell-tale signs of their husbands' infidelity. Then there are the selfish, character-flawed women who marry good men, who love and take care of them, but continue to consort with other men for sexual excitement or for the money and other material goods these men can provide.

In women's case, rather than being a loss of self-control when faced with an opportunity resulting from an undesirable or crabby husband, wives' infidelity is calculated and reflects a fundamental character flaw such as selfishness or materialism.

In sum, according to this website, men are "driven by desire" and a man is more likely to cheat if the other woman is "'hotter' than [his] wife or partner." Women, in contrast, are not motivated by sex, but instead are "lonely" or "selfish" despite their marriages to "good men." It's natural for men to want sexual variety and if there is a "better" sexual object available, they will be more motivated to stray, especially if their wives are not being "good"—that is, attentive and attractive. Women's reasons for cheating are more deeply psychological or even pathological.

Similarly, in an article published on the *Examiner* website (Houston 2011), the author lists the top ten reasons men and women cheat. For men, the reasons include, first, "more sex," followed by "sexual variety," "opportunistic sex," "to satisfy sexual curiosity," "to reaffirm his sexual-ity," "a feeling of entitlement," "the thrill of the chase," "ego embellish-ment," "peer pressure," and "sexual addiction." In contrast, the reasons women cheat include, first, "to fulfill an unmet need for emotional intimacy," followed by "dissatisfaction with her mate," "dissatisfaction with her marriage or relationship," "a desire for male attention," "reaf-firmation of her desirability as a woman," "to re-capture the feelings of romance or passion," "a desire to feel 'special,'" "boredom or loneliness," "feelings of neglect," and, last, "sexual excitement." The reasons men cheat are for the most part about sexual desire and sexual variety, while the reasons women cheat are relational, emotional, and bordering on pathological.

One reason cheating women are negatively perceived, harshly judged, and severely sanctioned might have less to do with their being disloyal to their husbands and more about their being disloyal to gender. By having sex or falling in love with a man other than her husband, a married woman refuses to play the complacent, controlled, and loyal wife and, instead, represents a form of pariah femininity.[5] "Cheating" is an expression of desire for another and requires agency in terms of planning, hiding, and lying. When a woman demonstrates the sexual subjectivity and agency required for cheating, it violates expectations for feminine sexuality. She is acting on her own desire, refusing to occupy the position of complacent companion, and therefore must be cast as a "bad woman."

In contrast, when a man "cheats" on his wife, the dynamics of an active masculine sexual subjectivity are "coupled" with a passive feminine sexual object in that the wronged wife has been replaced by a more desirable feminine object—the husband desires someone else. Mononormativity as it intersects with gender renders the cheating wife a flawed woman, while the cheating man is simply acting on his natural desire.

Moreover, the "good" woman whose husband cheats should "stand by her man," while no one would blame a man for leaving a cheating wife. After all, a cheating husband had a momentary loss of self-control, while a cheating wife is flawed. In fact, a man who doesn't leave a treacherous wife is emasculated even further, while a wife doesn't "lose" her femininity if she stands by her man and forgives him. It is not a coincidence that, in her polemic against monogamous love, Kipnis (2003) suggests that, regardless of who cheats on whom in a heterosexual couple, the cheating spouse is the "husband" and the wronged partner, the "wife" (16). To cheat is to act in a masculine way because it reflects desire and an active effort to fulfill that desire at the expense of others. To be cheated on is to be passive, cast aside as an undesirable sexual object. This means that, not only are individuals who cheat judged differently depending on their genders, the meaning structure of cheating as a social form is gendered.

Central to these narratives is the underlying assumption that men not only desire, but also *possess* the feminine sexual object.[6] A cheating wife casts doubt on her partner's ability to control her and situates her husband/partner in a hierarchical relationship with her lover. The lover "gets one over" on the cuckold by poaching or stealing his property. Fucking another man's wife is to gain power and status over that man. In her book *Open: Love, Sex, and Life in an Open Marriage*, Jenny Block (2008) describes a discussion she and her husband had about opening their marriage.[7] Her husband, Christopher, "admitted that one of his biggest concerns about [me having sex with other men] was that he'd walk into a restaurant one night and hear one guy say to another, 'I fucked that guy's wife.' . . . I would feel so stupid and small" (144). This quote captures how the betrayal of a cheating wife is not simply about the relationship between a husband and wife, it is also about the how the husband is situated as inferior to the other man because of the other man's access to "his" woman.[8] Perhaps this is why a woman who betrays her husband by having sex with another man, especially if that man is the husband's best friend, is so vilified.

I found myself in San Francisco on my way to meet Matthew[9] for a drink. It was all very "innocent" in the beginning. I was meeting Matthew because I had to pick up a painting he had completed for Ben, my lover and life partner and Matthew's best friend. Matthew is a handsome, intelligent artist, and while I found him attractive and always enjoyed his company, I never felt sexual desire for him. There just wasn't much chemistry. When I met him for a drink at a swanky wine bar, I had no intentions of having sex with him. It hadn't even crossed my mind.

Matthew greeted me with a platonic smooch on the lips and a long, warm hug. "Good to see you. Too bad Ben's not here, too."

I smiled, "I know. He's so jealous that I get to spend time with you and he can't."

We sat at the bar together and chatted about art while enjoying an over-priced but very good bottle of wine.

When the conversation turned to my and Ben's relationship, something changed. Feeling tipsy and losing inhibitions, we started talking about the ins and outs of our open arrangement of non-monogamy. Ben and I had agreed that sex with others was not only permitted, but also good for each of us as individuals and for our relationship.

As I answered Matthew's questions, the conversation turned to sex—my and Ben's sex. I wasn't sure how we ended up on that topic, but I started to notice those tingles that make me unconsciously hold eye contact a little longer, lean in a bit closer, and attend to the small detailed features of my interlocutor's face.

Matthew responded in kind, placing a casual hand on my thigh to emphasize the punch line of a joke or to punctuate an important point. I stared at his lips when he looked away to sip from his glass and, more than once, caught him doing the same. He wanted to hear the details of my sex life with Ben, and that made Matthew sexy. It was as if exploring the sex between Ben and me lit a fuse of erotic desire between us. The sparks spread along our flirtation, and neither one of us had any intention of dousing it.

My phone chimed, and hoping it was Ben so he could join our interaction, I lifted one eyebrow and reached into my purse. Matthew smiled and lifted his glass as if to excuse me and offer a toast in one gesture.

The text message was from my friend Jayne. "Where are you?"

I told Matthew that I had plans to meet a friend at another bar and that he should come with me. He was flattered to be invited and enthusiastically said he would follow me on his motorcycle. As I drove, I thought about Ben and about Matthew and about the last time the three of us were together.

Matthew had come to visit Ben and me in New Orleans. Ben had to work one evening, so Matthew and I went out to dinner together. We shared lots of laughter and good conversation, but there was no flirting, no desire, and certainly no physical contact.

After Matthew left New Orleans, Ben told me that he inadvertently saw an email Matthew was composing to a mutual friend. It said, "No one has tried to seduce me yet." Ben had told Matthew about the threesomes Ben and I had with other women and men, including the recipient of Matthew's email. Ben interpreted the email as an indication that Matthew was worried that we would try to seduce him. I wondered why he would be writing such a thing when Ben could (and did) see it and to a man with whom we had a threesome.

"Maybe he wants us to seduce him. Maybe that's why he came down for a visit," I suggested.

Ben scoffed, "No way. He was obviously relieved that we didn't try anything. Jesus, it never even crossed my mind to make a pass. That would just be weird."

I wasn't so convinced that Matthew was relieved rather than disappointed.

I looked in my rearview mirror at the single headlight of Matthew's motorcycle behind me. Aloud, I contradicted my initial assessment of Matthew and said, "He's kind of hot."

At the bar, Matthew, my friend Jayne, and I had an animated and sometimes contentious discussion about transgender identity and the difference between gender and sexual orientation. Matthew just couldn't wrap his mind around how a non-op transgender woman who is sexually involved with a ciswoman could be anything but a straight guy, let alone be a lesbian. Jayne, who is a lesbian-identified transgender woman involved with a ciswoman and who has a PhD in English literature tried to be patient, but couldn't help slipping in some rather dismissive, if not hostile, comments about Matthew's intelligence, or lack thereof. Matthew poked back, but there was no doubt that Jayne had the upper hand. She was frustrated but enjoyed using her intellectual claws to bat around Matthew like a confused mouse. Matthew played dumb and, I surmised based on his body language, had a hard-on. I interjected my two cents occasionally, but mostly I just watched Jayne top Matthew while Matthew practically giggled with glee. As I took in their serious and playful exchange, I decided that I wanted to fuck Matthew.

When Jayne left, Matthew and I moved from the table to the bar and scooted our stools so close to each other our knees were grazing each other's zippers. It didn't take long for the conversation to turn to whether or not we should become lovers. We agreed it probably would not be a good idea and then proceeded to stick our tongues down each other's throats.

A couple of hours later, I found myself in Matthew's bed sucking his cock like it was the last morsel of sexual sustenance in a post-apocalyptic erotic landscape. He had insisted on keeping the lights off so only the outside streetlamp illuminated our naked bodies in an urban, pink glow. I could barely see his face above me on the pillows, but I could hear him as he moaned. I take pride in my sucking skills, but I wondered if there might be something more going on. I imagined that he was imagining that I was Ben. Was I proxy for a homoerotic desire to be with Ben? Or was I a conduit to connect them in some queer kind of triangulation of desire?

When I climbed on top of him and asked if he had a condom, he said that he didn't want to have intercourse. "It wouldn't feel right because of Ben," he said as he pulled my pussy to his mouth and, with unexpected precision and passion, lapped me off while jerking his own orgasm with his hand.

When I dressed and left his apartment at 3 a.m., we kissed like when we greeted each other eight hours earlier. With a platonic peck on the lips and a long, warm hug, we said our goodbyes. When he pulled away, he said, "I don't think we should tell Ben. Let's keep this just between you and me. Okay?"

I was tired and wanted to leave, so rather than protest, I agreed, though I knew this really wasn't an option. Ben and I had few rules in our open relationship, but one of them was full disclosure and no secrets. As I drove the deserted, early morning streets of San Francisco, I decided I would call Matthew the next day and tell him that I was going to tell Ben when I returned to New Orleans.

I tried calling Matthew in the morning and got his voicemail. I left a message about how it was best to be honest with Ben and tell him about what happened, and that I'd like to talk about it. "Call me as soon as you can," was the last thing I said. Matthew didn't call back, and I returned to New Orleans the following evening.

When I walked in the home I shared with Ben, he was sitting on the sofa, his eyes were red and swollen from crying, and he didn't look up. Staring forward, he said, "I can't believe you would do this."

I knew exactly what he was talking about. "You talked to Matthew."

Then he looked up, his eyes hard. "You fucking lied to me."

"What do you mean, I lied to you?"

"We talked several times today on the phone and never once did you mention that you fucked my best friend."

"I didn't have a chance. I wanted to tell you in person, not on the phone."

"Bullshit. He told me about how you were not going to tell me. What the fuck? Fucking my best friend?"

"I didn't fuck him."

"Yeah, Matthew told me. You wanted to but he said 'no' out of respect for me."

For the first time, I regretted everything. Not because I chose to have sex with Ben's best friend. Neither one of us had ever placed off-limits boundaries around our friends. I regretted it because I was starting to realize what a fucking asshole Matthew was. "I understand how you feel betrayed, but could we talk about why I did it, what happened? What it means for us?"

Ben shook his head. "You really fucked up this time. You came between me and my best friend. I will never forgive you for this. Either you pack your shit and get out, or I will."

In the hall of shame and moral failing, there are few things worse than a woman seducing her lover's best friend. In a mononormative world, having sex with someone other than my partner is bad, but coming between my partner and his best friend through seduction makes infidelity with a stranger seem like forgetting an anniversary.

No one would blame Ben for being hurt and angry or for wanting to end his relationship with me. We take for granted the need for some sort of resolution to the "problem" that is erotic triangulation. Mononormativity and compulsory monogamy ensure, in fact demand that a man in

Ben's position end his relationship with such a treacherous woman and find another, more loyal partner.

This compulsory dyadic resolution to a WMM love triangle combined with the gendered construction of cheating wives as disposable pariahs allows (demands?) men an exit to establish a new monogamous couple. As Pepper Mint (2004) suggests,

> In a system of monogamy, any three-person situation is assumed to be unstable and short-term. Therefore, our culture considers a cheating situation to embody a competition between the faithful partner and the other lover. To the extent that the affair is successful or continues, the outside lover is seen as "winning," and the primary relationship is losing. If the affair is halted, the primary relationship wins, and the other lover loses. The end goal of the affair (and of the other lover) is supposedly to end the primary relationship and establish the affair as the new primary relationship. In other words, affairs are seen as an attempt to steal the cheating person. (63)

The only viable solution is a pairing off and reestablishment of the couple (me and Ben) or the friendship (Ben and Matthew).

Surely, we tell ourselves, it is natural that Ben feels betrayed and no longer capable of tolerating a relationship with me once I had sex with his best friend. After all, no man should be expected to "share" the woman he loves with any man, especially his best friend. Ben's reaction is understandable, if not expected.

But, *why*? Why is there, in contemporary U.S. culture, such a clear and compulsory injunction against men being at once best friends with each other and in an emotionally and sexually intimate relationship with the same woman?

Evolutionary anthropologists would argue that this taboo is "natural" in that it is an evolved, biological imperative. As the reigning paradigm in contemporary U.S. discourse, we are familiar with this explanation, but let me quickly lay it out.

According to evolutionary anthropologists, males invest a relatively small contribution to reproduction—copulation, ejaculation, and one sperm to fertilize an egg. Given this small investment into what could potentially lead to a rather large dividend—producing offspring with his genetic material—a man has little to lose and a lot to gain by copulating with as many women as possible.

Women, in contrast, invest a great deal of physical effort into producing one offspring—a limited number of eggs, one egg released per month, gestation, lactation, and child dependency for years—so their genetic interests lie in being extremely choosy when it comes to a mate. Women will find men with physical strength and the ability to provide resources and protection most appealing. So, while men's interests lie in copulating with as many women as possible, the survival of a woman's offspring depends on the father sticking around to provide resources and protection. In this way, men and women have evolved to have conflicting reproductive interests.

According to evolutionary anthropologists, men and women struck a bargain to resolve these conflicting interests through institutionalized, monogamous marriage. Because men do not want to invest time, energy, and resources into the survival of another man's offspring—no payoff for a big investment—they are sexually jealous and protective of the women with whom they mate. In exchange for their investment of resources and protection, men demand monogamy from women.

Monogamous marriage is an evolved compromise to compel men to provide for their offspring and for women to be monogamous. Women who were faithful and men who could provide were more likely to have their offspring survive, thereby passing into future generations the predisposition for men's sexual jealousy and women's desire for monogamous commitment. This is the reason, evolutionary anthropologists hypothesize, that in contemporary society, men crave sexual novelty and are prone to infidelity while demanding and enforcing monogamy on women. It is also the reason that most societies in the anthropological and sociological record have been either monogamous or polygynous (one man, multiple wives).

From an evolutionary anthropological perspective, Ben's jealousy and need to resolve the situation by ending his relationship with me is inevitable. Men naturally want to control and possess the sexuality of their mates in order to protect their genetic investments. Cultural taboos against "sharing" women and the social script for ending the relationship reflect a genetic predisposition for men to refuse to "share" women and for individual men to perceive any man who copulates with "his" woman as necessarily a genetic rival.

In the story above, Ben has to run off the rival/best friend, or he has to reject me and find someone more likely to produce his own offspring and protect his genetic investment. Ben's desire to resolve erotic triangulation through relationship dissolution resonates with and is a manifestation of an evolved human disposition for male sexual jealousy and female complicity and dependence. In sum, a woman having two or more husbands goes against evolved human nature, is reproductively maladaptive, and, given men's inherent sexual possessiveness, dysfunctional as an institutionalized form of marriage.

This evolutionary narrative would, of course, preclude polyandry—institutionalized marriage that includes one woman and multiple men. The empirical anthropological record, however, shows that institutionalized polyandry not only exists, it is found in every part of the world. The data on these societies suggest that women are perfectly capable of having more than one husband, male sexual jealousy is not inevitable, and "sharing" one woman works quite well in certain environmental, social, and cultural circumstances.

In a meta-analysis of polyandrous societies, Starkweather and Hames (2012) found that there are certain societal and demographic features that correlate with polyandry. These societies are more likely to be hunter-gatherer or foraging horticulturist than agriculturalist. This is important because during what evolutionary anthropologists call the environment of evolutionary adaptiveness (EEA), or the context in which we evolved to be human, humans lived in hunter-gatherer and foraging social groups. A skewed sex ratio and long-term male absence or high mortality rates for men also correlate with institutionalized polyandry but are by no means necessary for it. That is, there are polyandrous societies that do not have a skewed sex ratio where the men outnumber the women. Perhaps most important for my purposes here, Starkweather and Hames found that polyandry is more likely in egalitarian societies that do not have strict social hierarchies.

Moreover, empirical research on polyandrous societies shows that male sexual possessiveness and strict control of women's sexual behavior is not universal, and in fact, there are societies that do not have a word for sexual jealousy. Starkweather and Hames find that one of the main features of polyandry is the absence of or severe social sanctions for male sexual jealousy, even between men who are very close in terms of friendship or kinship.

In Inuit societies, for instance, spouse sharing is one of the central pillars of bonds between men. Starkweather and Hames write:

[Northern Alaskan] Inuit peoples have a variety of dyadic partnerships between men that are largely independent of kinship, such as seal-sharing, song, wrestling, and trading partnerships. These dyadic, non-kin relationships mark close social ties that appear to help buffer against risk in an environment in which resources may be scarce and close kin may not be able to help. In spouse sharing, reciprocal sexual access is permitted. . . . These relationships are expected to last a lifetime, children in the co-marriage group are not permitted to marry, and the couples establish strong bonds of friendship, mutual aid, and protection. . . . Among North Alaskan Inuit, most married couples were involved in such relationships. (165)

Similarly, there is evidence that the Shoshoni of west-central North America practiced polyandry and the anthropological data suggest that sexual jealousy was rare.

Interestingly, anthropologists who have studied the Shoshoni conclude that polyandry was possible and jealousy absent because of the absence of gender hierarchies of male dominance. Julian Steward (1936), the foremost anthropological expert on Shoshoni culture, writes,

> Shoshoni polyandry is intelligible only if regarded as the function of a social structure which did not contain factors to exalt man's position in the family. There was no excess of marriageable males produced either by female infanticide or by frequent polygyny, and, so far as can be determined, the ratio of men to women was not abnormal. There was merely an extraordinary simplicity of social structure which made the relationship of both sexes to plural marriage almost identical. (561)

He goes on to say, "Economic life, moreover, provided no property rights which gave either sex an advantage" (562). According to Steward, polyandry was a function of a gender egalitarian social structure in which men did not hold a superior position in the family, women's contributions to society were perceived as equal to that of men's, and there were no property rights that favored men. On jealousy, Steward concludes:

> These data seem to indicate that Shoshoni society was among the very few in the world in which the relative lack of female jealousy or importance, which makes polygyny so commonly possible, was matched by a comparable weakness of jealousy and importance in the male. Obviously, there must have been a tenuous development of that monopolistic feeling, that will to dominate, in the man, which, whatever be its true nature or explanation, in most cultures does not tolerate a rival in the home. (564)

Within this context of flat gender hierarchies, sexual jealousy among men (and women) was virtually nonexistent. Still, despite the empirical data, Steward is confounded by the lack of jealousy in Shoshoni men and contrasts it with the situation in "most" cultures, where men do not

"tolerate a rival in the home." Steward's conclusions cast Shoshoni polyandry as an aberration and, by doing so, he can sustain the evolutionary
narrative about the inevitability of male sexual jealousy despite empirical evidence to the contrary.

This approach to polyandry is common in evolutionary anthropology. To account for the existence of institutionalized polyandry, most
evolutionary anthropologists dismiss polyandrous societies as aberra-
tions, exclude them from the empirical data, or argue that polyandry
is not evolutionarily adaptive. Instead, they argue, polyandry is an ad-
aptation to extenuating, unnatural circumstances such as a complex
economic system (Symons 1979) or skewed gender ratios where men
outnumber women (Westermarck 1926), both of which did not exist in
the environment of evolutionary adaptativeness.

However, as described above, Starkweather and Hames's meta-analysis
reveals that, far from being an aberration, the number of polyandrous
societies is severely underestimated by evolutionary anthropologists.
Starkweather and Hames conclude that the wide variety of marriage
forms suggests that, though humans may have evolved to form intimate
sexual bonds of kinship, the form of those bonds—monogamous, polygynous, and/or polyandrous—are most likely cultural.

In their controversial book *Sex at Dawn*, Ryan and Jethá (2010) offer
an interesting reinterpretation of the same anthropological data to argue
that sexual promiscuity, not monogamy, is more likely our evolutionary
predisposition. Ryan and Jethá argue that, in the EEA, humans lived in
relatively small, close-knit nomadic groups that relied on interdepen-
dence and close communal ties. In that context, they suggest, competition for resources or for mates among adult males within the group
would be maladaptive. Rather than taking "ownership" of individual
women and their offspring, the group and individuals within the group
would be better served by cooperation and resource sharing.

According to Ryan and Jethá, sexual intimacy is an evolved and highly
effective way to develop bonds. If bonding with all members of the group
is necessary, it makes more sense that all of the women copulated with

all of the men rather than only one man. Not only would this eliminate in-group competition for mates, it would also result in all adults in the group perceiving all of the children as "their own" and working together to ensure their survival. In this counternarrative offered by Ryan and Jethá, the human female evolved to be promiscuous, not monogamous, and has a genetic predisposition to have emotional and sexual bonds with several males. Compulsory monogamy, they argue, emerged quite late in the evolutionary record and only as humans became sedentary agriculturalists and men developed an interest in holding on to their accumulated resources.

Among the evidence they offer to support their thesis, Ryan and Jethá discuss several cultures in South America that understand reproduction in terms of partible paternity. In cultures characterized by partible paternity, it is believed that, over time, semen accumulates to create the fetus. If a woman wants a baby with specific features (smart, brave, attractive, a good storyteller, etc.) she will have sex with a smart man, a brave man, a handsome man, and a man who can tell a good story so that her baby will have all of these desired characteristics. In other words, each man with whom a woman has intercourse adds something to the fetus, and all of the men who have sex with a woman are defined as the fathers of her child and share in the responsibilities of fatherhood. Far from institutionalizing monogamy to control and "own" the product of women's sexuality, in these cultures, sexual bonding is shared across men and women.

As a sociologist, I am neither very concerned with nor qualified to make claims about which evolutionary hypothesis, if either, is "correct." Instead, I am interested in *Sex at Dawn* as a discursive maneuver. As an extremely popular text outside of the academic discipline of anthropology[10] and highly controversial book within that discipline,[11] *Sex at Dawn* reveals both the mononormative and masculinist cultural bias operating in the paradigmatic and hegemonic assumption that men are naturally jealous, biologically predisposed to control women's sexuality, and crave sexual novelty, and the political stakes involved in the gender structure of The Monogamous Couple as an ideal. It offers a *polyqueer* intervention in the hegemonic and discursive anthropological construction of monogamy as a compulsory *and gendered* institution.

While jealousy and possessiveness seem "understandable" and "expected" and are labeled "natural" when it comes to WMM triangulation, the body of research on polyandry and highly politicized debates around *Sex at Dawn* suggest that there is something deeply social and cultural about the injunction against WMM triangulation. When we say it's "natural" for Ben to feel betrayed by his best friend and that there is an evolutionary or biological need to dissolve his relationship with me or his best friend, we are telling a story that reflects and maintains our own cultural assumptions about gender differences and monogamy.

In the story of Ben, Matthew, and me, it was the best friendship between Ben and Matthew that made sex between Matthew and me intolerable. Ben and I had an open relationship, and to some extent, Ben had, like other men in open relationships, reconfigured his sense of masculinity to not include a sense of proprietary control over me as his sexual partner. However, having sex with his best friend crossed a line that was not explicitly drawn or perhaps even consciously expected until I did it.

When the other man is the best friend, we focus on how it affects the friendship between the men and assume that the men's intimacy with each other is compromised. A fissure or cleave is *caused by* sexual intimacy with the same woman. They are pitted *against each other* in a way that separates them and that is incommensurate with being best friends. As Michael Kimmel (2008) suggests in *Guyland*, "Guys love girls—all that homosociality might become suspect if they didn't! It's *women* they can't stand. Guyland is the more grownup version of the clubhouse on *The Little Rascals*—the 'He-Man Woman Haters Club.' Women demand responsibility and respectability, the antitheses of Guyland. Girls are fun and sexy, even friends, as long as they respect the centrality of guys' commitment to the band of brothers" (13–14; italics in original). This would explain why two closely bonded heterosexual men must never be intimately and sexually involved with the same woman over time. It violates the bro code and allows a woman to come between best friends.

What if, however, this story, like the ones about cheating husbands and wives, is an ideological cover to mask the ways in which being lovers with the same woman conflicts with hegemonic masculinity? Perhaps the fissure between best friends is not *caused by* the sexual intimacy between a woman and a man's best friend, but instead, the compulsory cleave is a *remedy* to prevent the ways in which a shared lover might *change* the men's already established intimacy? Ben surely was capable of identifying with Matthew and could imagine me as a sexual object in relationship to Matthew's desire. Ben knows what it is like to have sex with me. He has intimate knowledge/memory of my body, my desires, my kinks, and my sounds, tastes, and smells. He can remember and therefore vividly imagine the sex Matthew and I had and situate himself in Matthew's place.

As discussed above, in a love triangle between two heterosexual men and a woman, there is a social interpretation and script available. Two desiring masculine subjects want the same object, and to the extent they want to possess that object over time and space, they are rivals.[12] Identifying with each other as desiring subjects in competition for possession of the same woman renders them equals as subjects and the woman as an object of competitive exchange. By sexually objectifying a "shared" woman, there is no risk of identifying with her as a desiring subject. The men's heterosexuality is secured by only identifying with each other as desiring subjects in relationship to a feminine sexual object. Because of the mononormative and gendered assumptions that one man has exclusive possession of one woman and other men who have sexual access to her are rivals, if Ben and Matthew want to remain best friends, they must agree that neither will possess me. I have to go. However, keep in mind that some cultures define mutual spouse exchange as an important aspect of intimacy and friendship between men. If "sharing wives" serves a social function in these cultures, it is likely that a strict prohibition in contemporary U.S. culture serves a function as well.

Let us, for a moment, suspend gendered mononormativity and imagine that Ben and Matthew remain best friends and my lovers over time.

Imagine, in other words, that we are in a polyamorous "Vee" and Matthew and Ben are not only best friends, but also metamours. Within the context of my ongoing, intimate relationship with Ben, and in the context of Giddens's pure relationships in general, I am not reducible to a sexual object but am, instead, an equal partner. As an equal partner, I can be a model for all sorts of things—as a devoted friend *and as a desiring subject in relationship to Matthew.*

After Matthew and I had sex, Ben was not just wrestling with the effects of my and Matthew's tryst on their friendship, he was also confronted with my desire for Matthew. When I had sex with Matthew, Matthew was no longer just a best friend; he was my lover and desirable when imagined by Ben from my perspective. I, the feminine object of exchange between supposed rivals (as defined in the cultural narrative that Matthew poached Ben's property and therefore necessarily becomes Ben's adversary), am the *desiring subject* and desiring both men, who are intimately, though not sexually, bonded with each other. Ben might ask himself, *what does she see in him? What was he like as a lover?* The same would be happening from Matthew's perspective in relationship to Ben. Because Ben and Matthew already love and respect each other as friends, it does not take much for either of them to actually see what I desire in the other. They become both desiring subjects and objects of desire *in relationship to each other* as long as I am a lover with both of them over time. In other words, an emotionally intimate polyamorous Vee involving two best friends and a woman opens up the possibility of identification with a woman as the desiring subject in relationship to a man and, as such, confounds the gender structure of identification and objectification.

As Marjorie Garber (2000) suggests, "some people . . . get involved in erotic triangles . . . because they like to change positions, especially across the gender and sexuality borderlines. It might seem as if this were a game that two could play as well or better than three, but with two there are only a pair of positions to choose from. . . . The permutations of three are both more numerous and more flexible. . . . The third (or fourth, or fifth, for 'three' is here a marker that means more than two) opens up the dyad toward the world" (431). If this is the case, and I believe that it is, a man who tolerates, or even embraces rather than fights or remedies WMM triangulation with his lover and best friend would have to reconfigure his masculinity—both in terms of a proprietary control over "his" woman *and* in relationship to another man as a desiring subject and a desirable sexual object. This might offer a theoretical explanation for Sheff's (2006) findings that polyamorous men experience a shift in their sense of masculinity, both in terms of letting go of feeling possessive and acknowledging their partners' desires for other men.

An emotionally intimate, polyamorous WMM triad opens up very interesting potentialities for queering heteromasculinity, even if the men are not sexually involved with each other. Perhaps the mere potential for reconfiguring heteromasculinity is precisely *why* there is a taboo against best friends being lovers with the same woman. In other words, the individual and collective intolerance of this situation exists not because WMM triangulation reduces intimacy between best friends. Instead, the situation is so problematic because it *changes* the intimacy between best friends, situating them *against each other* in a *queer* way. Once again, invoking Ahmed (2007) as I did in the previous chapter, to turn *toward* monogamy requires turning *away* from something else. When it comes to the taboo against best friends being lovers of the same women, that something else could be a rather queer bond between friends and a reconfiguration of masculinity.

WMM polyamorous relationship structures also have polyqueer implications for hetero-femininities. As I have shown above, monormativity is gendered in that promiscuity and/or having multiple partners is more acceptable for men than it is for women and men are expected to be possessive of and control their partners. Polyamory as a subculture rejects the double standard and condones multiple partners for women. Men are strongly discouraged from being jealous, possessive, and controlling of their partners. Released from the risk of slut shaming and the control of jealous partners, women feel a sense of freedom in terms of their own sexual subjectivity (Sheff 2005).

Moreover, as an alternative subculture (Schippers 2002), the relationship between hegemonic masculinity and femininity is reconfigured so heterofemininity is unmoored from devotion to one man and one man only (Robinson 1997). Though there are strong taboos against making explicit comparisons between partners in poly subcultures, the possibility is always there. Unlike compulsory monogamy, which eliminates the possibility that women could judge one man's sexual performance or the quality of the relationship with other men, polyamory introduces this as an everyday possibility. This translates into women's sense of entitlement to good sex, quality relationships, and the ability to make demands that are not "built" into the structure and expectations for monogamous heterosexual couple relationships (Sheff 2005).

Of course, there are heterosexual couple relationships that include good sex and communication and in which women can demand to have their needs met, and as Sheff (2005) found, there are poly relationships in which women take on an unfair share of emotional labor. However, as Cardoso et al. (2009) suggest, polyamory offers an opportunity to build relationships from the ground up, and for this reason, poly relationships, unlike monogamous ones, open up possibilities to remake the self. This, they argue, opens up opportunities for women (and men) to reconfigure gendered subjectivity and undo hegemonic relationships between and among femininities and masculinities.

Elisabeth Sheff (2013) finds in her research that the most stable poly relationship configuration is the WMM triad. Though this might seem contradictory to my claims here, I want to suggest that my theoretical framework offers two mutually supportive explanations for this finding. First, if my theory holds up, it would be difficult to get two straight-identified men to agree to the arrangement and thus require a great deal of communication and commitment to make it work. The WMM triads that make it through this transition would probably be very stable indeed. Second—and herein lies the crux of my theoretical argument—in order to enter into and sustain a WMM triad, the men would have to embody something other than hegemonic masculinity in terms of control and ownership of the woman, but also in the way they form intimate bonds with the woman and with the other man, their metamour. Perhaps these triads are so stable because, when each man accepts another man into their relationship, they reconfigure their masculinities to be less possessive, less controlling, more likely to identify with each other and with the woman partner, and ultimately *better partners*.

In a lingerie shop, I watched and listened while they wandered through the lace together with surprising comfort. Ben held up a pair of panties and looked them over. "Oh man, she'd look great in this."

Matthew reached to rub the lace between his fingers. "Yeah. I love this style. Hips covered in lace."

Ben shifted his eyes to Matthew's lips. "Oh, yeah. You pull the lace while I explore."

Matthew closed his eyes and took a deep breath. "White or black?"

Ben put his lips to Matthew's ear and whispered, "How 'bout the gray pinstripe?"

It seemed to take forever, but I waited. My hips ached as they fingered the lace and gently passed the image of my body back and forth to feed their desire for each other. It reminded me of the first time Ben and I had sex with Matthew. I was so willing to be led, to be the object in a way that would make Catharine MacKinnon cringe because she could never see what was happening between us as three.

Finally, with their arms full of panties, garters, and bustiers, the reluctant shopkeeper showed us to the back of the shop and into a private dressing room. They sat on a bench with their backs against a wall-sized mirror as I slipped behind the curtain.

While I removed my clothes and wiggled into the playfully masculine gray pinstripe panties and bustier, I listened to them rifle through boxes and bags. Adjusting in the mirror, I smiled when Ben said, "Oh my god, those shoes are so cute," and Matthew, now an excited schoolgirl, responded, "Oh my god, I know!"

One hip thrust out and one arm on the wall, I threw the curtain open. They looked up, each with one shoe in hand, mouths hanging open, and eyes wide. Matthew slid forward on the bench and reached for my hip. "Can I touch?" I gave him permission with my eyes. His fingers slid under the lace to caress my hip. "Oh yeah. This is nice." Ben came forward too.

Feigning modesty, I gently pushed their hands away. As I turned slowly and swung my hips away, they sighed. I glanced over my shoulder and pulled the curtain closed.

It was strangely quiet as I slipped out of gray sophistication and into the white, wedding-night virgin. I wondered what they were doing.

When I opened the curtain they were leaning forward, elbows on knees, chins in hand, eyes wide. They looked like naughty children waiting outside the principal's office. Their submission to anticipation struck me as funny, and I started to laugh.

Matthew's brow furrowed. "What? What's so funny?"

Ben looked at him and, realizing how silly they both looked, chuckled.

Matthew snapped, "What the fuck is so fucking funny?"

I stepped close and held his face in my hands down in front of the white lace. He lifted his angry and sexy eyes. "You are so cute," I whispered. "Do you know that? Do you know how fucking sexy and adorable you are? I love you so much."

And so it was said. I had not yet told Matthew or Ben that I love Matthew, but it was inevitable that it would come out eventually.

He lowered his eyes and contemplated my words now tangled in the lace. I didn't know how Ben might respond to my confession, so I glanced at him. He stared at Matthew with worried eyes.

Matthew looked up to me and a slow grin emerged in his eyes and spread to his lovely mouth. He reached over, took Ben's hand, and said, "I love you, too." Ben's eyes flooded with relief as he brought Matthew's hand to his mouth and kissed his fingers.

At the register, all three of us pulled out our wallets. The woman behind the counter looked up with some confusion, but then politely went back to packaging the goodies.

Ben had a higher income than Matthew and me combined and volunteered to pay. Both Matthew and I insisted we contribute something. After some negotiation, in which both Matthew and Ben requested that I not pay anything, they decided on a fair and proportional split.

After they paid, the woman stood with pursed lips, holding the packages above the counter. She looked at Ben, then to Matthew, and back to Ben. I looped my arm around Ben's. She smiled with relief and handed the bags to Ben. With a quick wink, she said, "For you, sir."

Ben smiled shyly. "Yes, for me," he said as he separated half of the bags and handed them to Matthew. "And for him, too."

The woman looked at Matthew, and Matthew winked. Her brow furrowed with confusion above her gold, bifocal glasses. We smiled, bid her thanks, and quickly made our way out to the street.

Several hours later, after many exchanges of panties and bodily fluids, we lay relaxed and entangled on the bed. I thought about how Ben and Matthew insisted on paying and how the woman handed the packages to Ben. I remembered the way she smiled at him, suggesting that the lingerie was really for him, for his pleasure, and then her confusion at the possibility that it was also for Matthew. Then I recalled the way each of them had relished the other tucked into lace and wondered what Adrienne Rich might have to say about it all. I giggled.

My lovers inquired with their eyes. I shrugged, "Oh nothing. Just thinking about how much I love that you love each other and are willing to share . . . your panties."

They both laughed. With a wry smile, Matthew said, "Maybe we should move to Utah and get married."

Ben lifted up on one elbow and looking across my body to Matthew said, "After what just went down, I'm not sure who would wear the wedding dress."

The mononormative stories we tell about WMM triangulation—that it naturally and inevitably situates man against man as rivals—conceal the potential for WMM triangulation to situate man against man in queer identifications and desires. In the "fantasy" narrative above, told with a polyqueer imaginary, unlike the initial story of rivalry between best friends and an expendable, treacherous woman, Matthew and Ben accept my love affair with the other, and by doing so, also form a sort of queer bond with each other as best friends.

The polyqueer narrative also raises questions about how accepting each other as both best friends and my lovers might transfigure not just their bond with each other and their sense of a gendered self, but also their sexual orientation toward objects of desire. Clearly, Ben and Matthew become sexually intimate in this narrative, exchanging bodily fluids[13] and panties. It would be easy to assume that they are bisexual or even "closeted" homosexuals given their willingness to enthusiastically fall into bed together.

To reiterate my theoretical claims in this chapter, they do not have "be" bisexual or homosexual to share and enjoy sexual and emotional intimacy with each other. Their desire for each other is a *result* of the cross-gender identification and sexual objectification necessary for cultivating the sexual and emotional intimacy between the three of us. In other words, they are neither bi nor gay; they are *polyqueer*.

Finally, polyamory allows individuals to partner with multiple people so, unlike in monogamous relationships, any one individual might have partners who differ from each other in significant ways. To the extent that we express and cultivate different aspects of our gendered selves in our interactions and relationships with other people, having multiple partners might open up an opportunity to do and embody gender in different ways in order to cultivate different ways of knowing and doing (Schippers 2012).

For example, I grew up in a "mixed-class" family. My mother is from an upper-class family of business entrepreneurs. Her father and her siblings have summer homes in rural Wisconsin, and as the daughter of a wealthy businessman, my mother expected to be economically dependent on and well provided for by my father.

My father, in contrast, has working-class origins. He lived much of his childhood in a single-mother home. His uncles, cousins, and brothers were firefighters, police officers, and electricians. Though my father has a post-graduate education, he has a strong working-class sensibility and disdains anything that smacks of upper-class sensibilities or extravagances.

Because my parents came from very different class backgrounds, and despite my father's upward mobility through his profession, my immediate family was inter-class in terms of habitus. We had a large home in the suburbs and a summer home, as well—something my paternal extended family didn't have—but we never ate at restaurants, took extravagant vacations, or had expensive, designer clothing—luxuries my maternal extended family took for granted. Class anxieties and animosities were present much of the time for my parents and thus for me, and especially when choosing to spend time with extended family. In other words, I grew up with an acute sense of class bifurcation.

One of my partners, I'll call him Samuel, has upper-middle-class origins, makes an upper-middle-class living, and embodies an upper-middle-class habitus. Chris (also a pseudonym), my other partner, comes from a rural, working-class background, makes a working-class wage, and embodies a rural, working-class habitus. When I was partnered with both of them, my "bi-class" subjectivity and habitus no longer felt like a split or betrayal to one side of my family or the other.

With Samuel, I could cultivate and play with aspects of my femininity by shopping for clothes and eating at expensive restaurants and, because of our differences in income and because gender play was one our favorite games, letting him pay. I could also get my masculinity on when we went mountaineering or rock climbing in foreign countries or when training together for triathlons.

Spending time with Chris was different. Neither one of us could afford expensive restaurants unless it was a special occasion, and we had to save to take vacations together. But I did not want to do those things with Chris. They just were not part of our habitus when we were together. Instead, Chris and I spent our time walking in a forest, going to see a movie, or staying in to spend hours on a home-cooked meal and playing board games. With Chris, I often felt like masculinity and femininity temporarily slipped away from or below the surface of what we were doing together.

At the same time, as metamours, Samuel and Chris were exposed to each other and their differences in ways they might not have had they not both been partnered with me. The three of us did not spend a whole lot of time together, probably at least partially because of their differences in class habitus, but they nonetheless communicated with each and honored my desire to be with the other in ways that worked for all of us.

What implications might this have for children with parents of different races? How might metamour relationships across race and class difference facilitate cross-race identification while not erasing important and valued differences? Many have written about how polyamory makes bisexuality visible because one can be simultaneously partnered with people of different genders, but what about "bi-racial" or "bi-class" subjectivity or metamour relationships across class and race difference? Perhaps polyamory as a relationship form not only offers potentialities to open up new gendered subjectivities; it might also open potentialities for identification and bonding across race and class differences.

2

Black Respectability in a Perfect World

The "Down Low," Polyamory, and Bisexuality in E. Lynn Harris's Invisible Life

My sleep was interrupted with a dream of Quinn and Nicole. In the dream they were each pulling me in a different direction. I awoke before I found out in which direction I ended up going. (227)
—Raymond Tyler in *Invisible Life*, by E. Lynn Harris

In 2012, R&B artist Frank Ocean released his first solo recording. In the liner notes, he refers to having been in love with a man. The mainstream media picked up on this as an example of a black hip hop artist "coming out as gay." Ocean never said he was gay; he said he had once been in love with a man. Touré (2012) writes in a *Time* magazine article, "Where [white, upper-class Anderson] Cooper talks about it as an almost clinical fact about himself—'I'm gay, always have been, always will be'—Ocean takes a much more nuanced view by describing a pivotal relationship, never attaching a label to himself." In a short essay published in the anthology *Recognize: The Voices of Bisexual Men*, Rodney McGruder Brown (2014) writes, "Coming out as a BBM (Black Bisexual Male) is one of the most important things that I have ever done in my life. My process of coming out of the closet began when I was about 13 and I realized that my attraction to guys was the same as my attraction to girls. This attraction included emotional and sexual attraction" (13). He explains how he first interpreted his feelings for guys as "extreme admiration, but never admitting to a genuine attraction" (13). The shame and confusion he felt about his desire for men *and* women was the "result of being taught that sexuality is black and white, gay or straight. I began to ask myself whether I was attracted to men or women. I did not want to identify as straight and I did not want to identify as gay. I had trouble with identifying as gay because I was still very much attracted to women" (13).

Raymond Tyler Jr. is an upper-middle-class, professional black man who, like Rodney McGruder Brown, "did not want to identify as straight and . . . did not want to identify as gay." In the dream described above, Quinn, his lover, and Nicole, the woman he wants to marry, pull him in what appear to be separate directions. In one direction is the identity *gay black man* and in the other is the heteronormative life of a *respectable black man*, or so is Raymond's dilemma, described in E. Lynn Harris's *Invisible Life.*, The first book in a trilogy, *Invisible Life* is a fictional narrative of Raymond Tyler's struggle with choosing between what he calls a "gay lifestyle" on the one hand or living the respectable life of marriage, church, and professional success on the other, for he cannot envision having both.

Written in the late 1980s and self-published in 1991, *Invisible Life* was, according to Harris, largely autobiographical and is considered one of the first published accounts of a black man on the "down low" or "DL." In a collection of novellas written in tribute to Harris, Terrance Dean (2010) writes, "How did he understand how it felt to be caught like this, between two worlds, heterosexual and homosexual? Like Raymond, and like thousands of men, I later discovered, I felt like an anomaly. There were so many of us, and we all felt uniquely burdened and isolated. But that summer, after reading Harris's breakthrough novel, I felt I was not alone" (1–2). Dean goes on to write, "For the first time he gave [black women] a glance into a hidden world of intricate and compelling love stories between athletes and professionals, gays and men on the down-low" (2). In the same volume, James Earl Hardy (2010) writes, "There will be those who bite, mimic, imitate, and copy his storytelling technique and style, but no one will ever be able to reproduce or repeat it, or have the cultural impact he had" (126). The novel *Invisible*

Life is credited by these authors and others with being the first narrative account and accurate portrayal of the emotional, sexual, and political dilemma between the straight life of respectability and accepting the identity "gay" for black men who have sex with women and men (MSWM).

"On the DL" is a colloquial term that emerged in the African American lexicon to refer to any covert sexual behavior and was picked up by the mainstream media to refer specifically to African American men who identify as heterosexual, maintain relationships with women, and secretly have sex with men.[1] Over a decade after the publication of *Invisible Life*, J. L. King (2004) published a "tell all" confessional about his own life on the DL. According to King, a man is on the DL when he regularly engages in sexual relations with other men but (1) does not identify as gay, (2) maintains intimate and sexual relationships with women, and (3) is not "out" about his desire for and sexual relationships with men. According to King, the DL is not uncommon among African American men, and in his alarmist treatise, King casts men on the DL as duplicitous, selfish, and responsible for introducing and spreading HIV to African American populations.

Unlike E. Lynn Harris, who was never taken up as a mainstream media sensation, J. L. King became a regular guest on talk shows, appearing more than once on *Oprah*. In King's wake, a mainstream media storm blew up around this phenomenon called the "down low." *Invisible Life*, a beautifully written, poignant, and apparently realistic narrative about not just sexual desire, but also a deep longing for and experience of emotional intimacy with women and men, was eclipsed by King's sensational caricature of and warnings about compulsive and selfish black men on the DL. While both texts address the transmission of HIV from men on the DL to unsuspecting women in African American communities, Harris's novel focuses on Raymond's love for the women and men in his life and how this precludes living a respectable life, while King focuses on sex, dishonesty, and the threat the black man on the DL poses to African American women.

Demonized as the source of the increased rate of HIV infection among heterosexual women, African American MSWM, as a group, were suddenly placed in the spotlight. Much of this public discourse about men on the DL cast them as closeted gay men incapable of admitting that they are gay and trying to "pass" as straight. Joy Marie (2008) joined J. L. King in sounding the alarm to African American women about men on the DL. The preface to her polemical book *The Straight-Up Truth about the Down-Low* (2008) begins with this paragraph:

> Imagine . . . You have finally met Mr. Right. He's everything you dreamed of: handsome, sexy, charming, intelligent, articulate, and financially successful. He even portrays the role of and excellent father. He does not smoke, drink, or use drugs and he has a decent credit history. You marry him and buy your dream house in the suburbs. Your children attend the best schools and you live in a *wonderful* neighborhood. You're finally living the American dream—the perfect family—but one day you wake up and realize that your Prince Charming is really a lying Queen. (xi; italics in original)

This quote juxtaposes "Mr. Right," the embodiment of a respectable black man, with its antithesis, the "lying queen" or closeted homosexual. She goes on to write, "From our research, we have discovered there is really no difference between Black men being on the down-low and any other men being in the closet—they are *all* closeted homosexuals" (3).[2]

Casting MSWM as "closeted" gay men, castigating them for lying about it while maintaining relationships with wives and girlfriends, and insisting they just "come out" and stop cheating is a *monormative* narrative as well as a heterosexist one. A respectable black man is, by definition, middle class, a good father, but also and necessarily, one hundred percent heterosexual *and faithful*. Without diminishing the pain of infidelity experienced by Joy Marie, her virulent biphobia and erasure of queer desire takes shape as anger over being lied to and cheated on. This is clear when she lists the "tell-tale signs a man is on the DL" and writes, "Admits to being bisexual (he's gay)" (91). The problem is not that men on the DL have homosexual desire; the problem is that they are not honest with themselves and others about being gay, refuse *to choose*, and continue to have sex with men while maintaining relationships with women.

While King and Joy Marie focus on the duplicity of individual men on the DL, the mainstream media constructed the DL as a problem endemic to African American cultures and communities (Bryant and Vidal-Ortiz 2008; Vidal-Ortiz 2008). As meticulously reported by Keith Boykin (2005) in his acclaimed book *Beyond the Down Low*, much of the mainstream discourse around African American MSWM was negative and focused on homophobia on the part of both the men who were having sex with women and men—they couldn't just admit they are gay—and on the assumed heterosexism endemic to African American communities. If black churches did not spread homophobia and heterosexism, the narrative went, these men could embrace their true identity as gay black men and stop deceiving African American women (Decena 2008). In one stroke, both African American culture and the supposedly closeted, gay black men who couldn't just admit it were cast as homophobic *and* (ir)responsible for the spread of HIV (Ford et al. 2007). Keith Boykin writes, "For white America, the down low is a way to pathologize black lives. And for the media, the down low is a story that can be easily hyped" (21). The "black man on the down low," as a media-constructed *representation* of sexualized African American masculinity was a new form of an old pattern of constructing African American sexual norms, ethics, and behaviors as a social problem.

The Politics of Respectability and Monogamous Marriage

Pathologizing the real or imagined sexual practices of African American women and men has a long history in the U.S. and is a central feature of racial formation and white supremacy. Patricia Hill Collins (2005) identifies the contours of what she calls black sexual politics or

representations of African American sexuality as primitive, pathological, and/or a social problem. According to Collins,

> Black sexual politics consists of a set of ideas and social practices shaped
> by gender, race, and sexuality that frame Black men and women's treat-
> ment of one another, as well as how African Americans are perceived
> and treated by others. Such politics lie at the heart of beliefs about Black
> masculinity and Black femininity, of gender-specific experiences of Afri-
> can Americans, and of forms that the new racism takes in the post-civil
> rights era. (7)

Collins suggests that gender constructions, specifically racialized and
sexualized cultural constructions of masculinities and femininities, are
a central feature of new racism. Controlling images of African American
women as promiscuous, bad mothers, and, more recently, the "educated
bitch" and of African American men as sexually predatory athletes and
criminals, sidekicks, or "sissies" situate white masculinities and femininities as normal, moral, and civilized.

In efforts to combat representations of African American sexuality
as inferior to white, many African Americans embraced what Evelyn
Brooks Higginbotham (1993) calls a politics of respectability. Coming
largely out of the black Baptist church and women activists fighting both
racism and sexism, a politics of respectability is simultaneously the radical assertion that black women deserve the respect of white women and
a call to African Americans to live up to the ideals of Victorian white
society.

> Respectability demanded that every individual in the black community
> assume responsibility for behavioral self-regulation and self-improvement
> along moral, education, and economic lines. The goal was to distance
> oneself as far as possible from images perpetuated by racist stereotypes.
> Individual behavior, the black Baptist women contended, determined the
> collective fate of African Americans. It was particularly public behavior

that they perceived to wield the power either to refute or confirm stereo-
typical representations and discriminatory practices. . . . There could be
no laxity as far as sexual conduct, cleanliness, temperance, hard work,
and politeness were concerned. There could be no transgression of society's norms. (196)

Respectable men work hard to become economically successful enough
to support a family, and they are active in community affairs and faithful
to family and church. A respectable woman is a good mother, especially protective of her sons, supportive of her husband and household,
religious, and sexually pure.[3] As prescriptions for how to be a man or
woman within the context of the family, respectability is at once resistance to white-supremacist constructions of the pathological African
American family (see chapter 1) and sexualities, and a race-specific
manifestation of the heterosexist and male-dominant nuclear family.

Black nationalism in the 1960s and 1970s picked up the politics of
respectability and reinforced the idea that men's and women's respec-
tive roles were key to advancing and uplifting African Americans and
fighting white supremacy. Insisting that women's role was to support
black men, many black nationalist leaders emphasized domesticity and
faithfulness to the black man for women. Trimiko Melancon (2014) calls
this "the classical black female script" and defines it as "constituted by
black women's expected racial loyalty and solidarity, sexual fidelity to
black men, self abnegation, and idealization of marriage and mother-
hood" (49).

Dwight McBride (2005) suggests that the politics of respectability,
as heterosexist and dependent on hegemonic forms of masculinity and
femininity, resulted in the exclusion of African American gay men and
lesbians. He writes, "the politics of black respectability . . . can be seen
as laying the foundation for the necessary disavowal of black queers in
dominant representations of the African American community, African
American history, and African American studies" (38). From McBride's
perspective, definitions of respectability within the African American

community are heterosexist in that they assume and perpetuate the idea that homosexuality is contradictory to black identity. Unlike mainstream media narratives of the DL that explain the secrecy of African American MSWM as the manifestation of homophobia endemic to the religiosity of African American culture, McBride contextualizes heterosexism as part and parcel of not religiosity, but instead of a politics of respectability that emerged in response to white-supremacist racial formation.

Without dismissing or denying the heterosexism of the politics of respectability, I want to suggest that "no transgression of society's norms" includes embracing and practicing not just heterosexuality, but also monogamy. The faithful and committed husband challenges the controlling image of black men as incapable of monogamy, ill suited for long-term relationships, and/or passively tolerant of cheating wives, and the sexual purity of the African American wife contradicts racist representations of black women as sexually promiscuous, licentious, and available. Respectable masculinities and femininities, like the hegemonic masculinities and femininities associated with whiteness discussed in chapter 1, manifest as structures for ethical and moral relationships and sexual intimacy. Respectable intimate relationships are *both* heterosexual *and* monogamous, and African American MSWM violate *both* heteornormativity *and* mononormativity.

The "Normal" Gay, Monogamy, and the Black Man on the DL

Similarly to the ways in which black respectability was adopted by African Americans to resist controlling images of racialized sexualities, white gay men adopted their own politics of "normal" to resist the controlling images of gay men that emerged with the HIV epidemic (Warner 1999). Initially assumed to be largely a white gay men's problem, much of the public discourse circulating about HIV focused on the absence of monogamy in gay men's culture. In response, a gay politics of "normalcy" emphasized (1) "coming out" or publicly self-identifying as gay, (2) safer sex practices, and (3) monogamy. As middle-class, white, and gender-conforming gay men publicly and vociferously advocated safer sex practices and monogamy and lobbied for the right to serve in the military and access to marriage, the DL emerged as a social problem indicative of not just homophobia in the black community, but also the uncontrolled promiscuity and duplicity of young African American men "on the down low." The moral panic around HIV was not, in other words, just about homosexuality, it was also about race and non-monogamy.

The Black Man on the DL, as a socially constructed, controlling image of African American sexualized masculinity emerged contemporaneously with the HIV epidemic and moral panics around sexual promiscuity (Boykin 2005; Sandfort and Dodge 2008). As a representation of black masculinity, the "DL" was intelligible in relationship to both the politics of black respectability *and* white homonormativity. If we weave a relational web[4] rather than view the black man on the DL in isolation, we can better understand how this representation of a racialized masculinity is situated in between those of the *respectable black man* and the *normal gay* and serves as an abject other to both. The respectable black man is honest, heterosexual, and monogamous while the black man on the DL is duplicitous, closeted, and promiscuous. In this binary construction, morality hinges on *both* heterosexuality *and* fidelity.

At the same time, within the context of the HIV epidemic and its discourses, representations of the *gay white man* served as the scapegoat for HIV, and anxieties about and moral panics over the spread of the disease were placed on the bodies of men who fit that image. Through a similar logic of morality hinging on heterosexuality and monogamy, the main difference between the straight white man as moral and the gay white man as abject other was not just a hetero/homo distinction; it was also a monogamous/promiscuous difference. To combat the heterosexist, misinformed, and dangerous assumptions about HIV epidemiology and prevention, lesbian and gay activists challenged these controlling images by coming out as gay and advocating, if not safer sex practices, then monogamy.

I want to suggest that the black man on the DL served as a discursively constructed abject other that, at least in part, rendered gay pride (including publicly claiming the identity) and a desire for monogamous marriage as moral and superior to being "in the closet" and non-monogamous. The gay white man is, in this logic, intelligible as a moral citizen in his difference from the closeted and promiscuous black man on the DL.

As homosexuality was politicized and the LGBT rights movement gained a foothold, the problem of the DL was a convenient foil for the "normal" homosexual who accepted and celebrated (1) a homosexual identity and (2) the heteronormative, monogamous family.

The image of the black man on the down low is, in other words, another example of racial formation that conflates whiteness with morality and blackness with immorality. Central to my purposes here, this binary hinges on neoliberal identity politics that conflate "coming out" with morality, but also, and importantly, the conflation of morality with monogamy. The black man on the DL was "confused" or "closeted" while the homonormative gay white man was "born this way," out, and proud, and the black man on the DL was promiscuous while the gay white man was monogamous.

As anxieties about promiscuity in white gay male culture were displaced on to the bodies of young, urban black MSWM, black respectability and homonormativity became intelligible in their difference from the black man on the DL as the abject *promiscuous* other. The black man on the DL was defined through a relational web of race, gender, and sexuality that hinged on the conflation of monogamy with honesty, morality, and responsibility and contrasted with non-monogamy as duplicitous, immoral, and irresponsible.

If, however, we shift our attention from media-constructed representations of the black man on the down low to sociological and public health research on African American MSWM, a different picture emerges. Without denying that internalized homophobia probably plays some role in some individuals' secrecy about having sex with men, when asked about their sexual identities, practices, and experiences, African American and Latino men describe their sexual practices as pleasurable and convenient given their social location. Latino and black MSWM have intimate and sexual relationships with women and want to continue to do so. Many insist that sex with men is pleasurable and more convenient than sex with women because women require more emotional work and time for sexual access. While some use the label "bisexual" to describe their sexual orientation, most do not. They reject the common assumption in both heteronormative and homonormative cultures that bisexuality is simply a phase or transition to coming out as gay or a desire to keep one foot in heterosexual privilege.

At the same time, many of these men reject the idea of having been "born that way" and refuse to define themselves as "gay" or "homosexual" (Malebranche et al. 2009) because the label "gay" is synonymous with whiteness and middle-class status. They talk about how embracing a gay identity would mean rejecting their own cultures and communities to join an unwelcoming, racist, and class-privileged culture. While much of the mainstream media reduced the DL to internalized homophobia and heterosexism in African American and Latin communities, there was little discussion of the racism of white, middle-class gay communities, and perhaps equally important, the biphobia of white, middle-class gay men and African American women. Some African American MSWM go so far as to insist that having sex with black men rather than white gay men is a form of race and gender solidarity, a sort of same-gender loving as described by Trimiko Melancon (2014).

Finally, African American and Latino MSWM also reject the label "gay" because they understand being gay to mean being "punk" or sissy (Fields et al. 2012). For these men, "gay" or "homosexual" is equated with femininity, and because the participants in this research see themselves as masculine, they say that the label "gay" does not make sense to them.

Though this research is more sympathetic with Latino and black MSWM's rejection of a gay or bisexual identity and allows for a somewhat "quare" (Johnson 2001) reading of DL culture and practices, a focus on homoerotic desire alone misses a crucial aspect of DL culture—that is, a desire for and insistence on *non-monogamy*. As a sexual culture, the DL is an unapologetic rejection of heteronormativity, homonormativity, *and* mononormativity. The cacophony of stigmatizing rhetoric told black men on the DL to be *either* respectable black men *or* "normal" gay men. While this reflects and rearticulates a heterosexual/homosexual binary—respectable black men are heterosexual while gay black men are homosexual—it also reveals an underlying insistence that all respectable men, regardless of sexual orientation, stay faithful to both sexual identity and their partners.

It is in this world that E. Lynn Harris situates Raymond Tyler's struggle to be a respectable black man. Focusing less on Raymond's sex life and more on his desire for intimacy, *Invisible Life* offers a view of the DL as a *relationship orientation toward plurality* as much as a sexual orientation toward women and men. In the novel, Raymond Tyler does not struggle with shame about homoerotic desire; he struggles with being in love with more than one person in a world that demands that he choose one or the other.

Below, I will offer a *polyqueer* reading of *Invisible Life* to reveal and demonstrate that Raymond Tyler's desire is to love and have a committed, *polyamorous* relationship with both Quinn and Nicole while maintaining his status as a respectable black man. Raymond's story, I argue, is a polyqueer narrative of an African American man "on the down low" in that it is a *social* critique of compulsory monogamy and mononormativity as much as it is a critique of heteronormativity and homonormativity. At the same time, as a polyqueer text, it offers, in Raymond's dream of a perfect world, a glimpse into the potential for polyqueer sexual subcultures like the DL to transfigure notions of masculinity, render visible male bisexual desire, and change relationships between and among women and men.

The Polyqueer Life of Raymond Tyler Jr.

Raymond Tyler Jr. is a respectable black man who finds himself in sexually and emotionally intimate relationships with women and men. While the entire world, both academic and non-academic, focuses on the homoerotic sexual experiences of men on the DL, in E. Lynn Harris's telling, Raymond's struggle is first and foremost with loving two people at the same time and feeling that he must choose between them. Raymond aspires to be and eventually becomes a respectable black man and succeeds in every way except one: he is lying to the world about his relationships and sexuality. As I will show below, he is dishonest, not because of internalized homophobia or shame about his desire and love for men; he is on the DL because he knows that in a *biphobic and mononormative* world, his goals in life—to be a family man, professionally successful, and active in his church, and to give back to the community by getting elected to public office—would be impossible if he were honest with his lovers and the world about his desire to be polyamorous.

The novel begins with Raymond reading a letter that ends with, "Why can't we live in a perfect world?" After he reads the letter, Raymond asks himself, "How did this happen?" The reader is then taken on a journey through Raymond's recollection of the past to explain how he ended up where he is. "Why can't we live in a perfect world" sets up the narrative as less a psychological journey, although that is certainly a component to the story, and more a critique of the world around him—the social world in which he could not fit—and a desire for something different.

Sela and Kelvin

Raymond starts his story at the beginning of his senior year in college when everything, it seems, is perfect. The son of hard-working parents who managed to climb into the middle class, Raymond is smart, industrious, and ambitious, and his ambition is very much tied to class mobility. He is a member of Kappa Alpha Omega (KAU), one of three black fraternities on campus. To honor one of their advisors, the fraternity plans to hold a party at the home of "one of the few black faculty members at the university" (4). Raymond describes the professor's house as "a huge old rustic house outside of town surrounded by trees so large they cast an indelible shade over the two tennis courts and aqua-colored pool. It was the type of house I dreamed of one day sharing with Sela" (4).

Sela is Raymond's college girlfriend. Placing Sela so centrally in his dreams and aspirations sutures long-term, monogamous heterosexual marriage with Raymond's ideas of success. Raymond describes her as she arrives at the fraternity.

> Sela looked beautiful in her white tennis outfit. It was a pleated short skirt with a matching top that looked wonderful against her vanilla wafer brown complexion. Her long black hair was pulled together with a crimson stain ribbon that flowed down her back. Her face, with deep dimples and almond-shaped, hazel eyes, was accented by an open smile. (4)

Sela embodies the perfect complement to Raymond's upper-middle-class masculinity. The tennis outfit, a signifier of class, looks "wonderful" against her light skin, long black hair, and hazel eyes. Not only are Sela's physical features and hobbies a perfect complement to Raymond's visions for the future, she is Southern and from an upper-middle-class family who "surprised her for Christmas with a new Ford Mustang" (31). The Raymond we meet at the beginning of the story is the embodiment of respectable masculinity—a young man who aspires to be a professionally successful family man, and appears to be poised to make this happen.

It is at a Kappa Alpha Omega party that Raymond first sees Kelvin, the man with whom he has his first same-gender loving relationship and who introduces Ray to DL culture. Raymond notices how Kelvin, at this point no more than a handsome stranger, attracts the attention of women. Based on his appearance, mannerisms, and dance moves, Raymond concludes that the stranger is "east Coast *for real*" (7). The next day, on a flight to New Orleans to attend a cousin's wedding, Raymond dreams about the man he saw at the party.

> I had a dream that bothered me. I didn't quite remember all the details, but the stranger from the party the night before was in it. He was visiting the campus to see if he might want to come to school next year. All during my stay in steamy New Orleans I thought about the dream. I was puzzled as to why I was dreaming about a guy I had seen only once and to whom I had never spoken a word. My return flight to school went smoothly and didn't include any illusions about the stranger or Sela, whom I dreamed of often when we were separated. (8)

Reflecting on the dream, and puzzled by it, Ray is relieved that he dreams about neither Sela nor the stranger on his flight home. The stranger occupies the same corner of his consciousness as Sela, his girlfriend and lover. Though Raymond dreams about her "often," his relief raises the specter of internal conflict about his feelings for the stranger and his relationship with Sela. Here we see the beginnings of triangulation between Sela, who represents the respectable life Ray desires, and the stranger, a man with whom he will eventually fall in love. This is a consistent pattern in the book. Each time Raymond feels a conflict between being a respectable black man and being sexually and emotionally involved with men, love for and attraction to a woman creates a dynamic of triangulation. He is not simply pulled in one direction (respectability) or another (homosexuality); he is caught in the middle, because he loves two people.

A few months later, Raymond sees the stranger again in the gym locker room. After a brief exchange in which Kelvin asks to borrow a comb and unabashedly stares at Ray, Kelvin asks where he can buy liquor. When Raymond tells Kelvin he would have to drive thirty-five miles to the nearest liquor store, Kelvin says, "[T]his place is different." Raymond asks where he is from. Kelvin tells him Philadelphia and that he is going to school on a football scholarship. As an athlete from the northeast on scholarship, Kelvin embodies a contrast to the respectable masculinity of Raymond, an academic achiever from Birmingham, Alabama.

Kelvin then asks Raymond if he would give him a ride to the liquor store. Raymond agrees, and on his way to pick up Kelvin, takes a detour to Sela's sorority to see if she wants to go with them. En route, he thinks about the dream he had about Kelvin. Again, in Ray's consciousness, Sela is situated in direct relationship to Kelvin. He experiences a desire to include her at the same time he remembers his dream about Kelvin. Upon finding out Sela is not available to go with them, Raymond and Kelvin drive to the liquor store alone. During the ride, Raymond feels "uneasy" because Kelvin stares at him and looks him "straight in the eyes" while they talk about "sports, school and, of course, females" (11).

After picking up beer, they eventually end up at Raymond's apartment, where Kelvin reveals that he is "bisexual." When Ray refers to "sissies" in high school, Kelvin angrily says, "Do I look like a sissy to you?" (14). Like the Latino and African American men described in the research literature on MSWM, Kelvin insists that his being bisexual is distinct from being a "sissy" in order to make clear that he is not gay.

Kelvin also suggests that having sex with men does not negate his desire for women. Raymond asks, "Don't you like girls?" and Kelvin responds, "I love women. Nobody eats trim better than me . . . you know, pussy" (15). Shocked, Raymond asks, "[W]hy in the fuck would you want to mess around with a man?" Calmly and confidently, Kelvin says, "Variety is the spice of life." When Raymond says he has never "made it with a guy," Kelvin suggestively states, "Maybe you haven't run across the right man" (15).

In their first meeting, Kelvin introduces Raymond to DL cultural understandings of gender, sexual identity, and sexual behavior, including the ideas that (1) having sex with women does not exclude the possibility of having sex with men, (2) being a skilled lover with women is consistent with rather than contradictory to his desire for men, and (3) despite having a girlfriend and never having "made it with a guy," Raymond might find "the right man" in Kelvin.

During this conversation, Raymond notices that Kelvin has an erection, and after nervously suggesting they get back to campus, Kelvin moves in to kiss Raymond. Raymond describes how he is overcome with desire.

> I couldn't believe it, but it felt so natural. It was the first time I had ever kissed a man. I had never felt a spasm of sexual attraction toward a man. Honest to God. But his kiss. I had never kissed anyone like this, not even Sela. Before I was conscious of it, I was kissing Kelvin back and putting my arms around his waist. His force left little room for hesitation or resistance. I felt his strong body press toward mine—and an erection in my Jockey underwear, just aching to come out. I finally managed to pull back when I realized my sex was now full and hard, pressing against my navel. Kelvin looked down at me, gave a half-cocked grin and then pulled me toward him once again. This time there was no resistance. (16)

Kissing Kelvin's "strong body" was different from kissing Sela, and Kelvin's "force left little room for hesitation or resistance." Though he had never "felt a spasm of sexual attraction toward a man," this first kiss with Kelvin opens Raymond to the experience of feeling homoerotic desire.

Rather than having been "born this way," Raymond describes his desire for Kelvin as something that emerges through embodied experience rather than a hidden and essential part of self.

> On that night, the first Friday in October, I experienced passion and sexual satisfaction that I had never in my twenty-one years dreamed possible. Until that Friday evening in October, sex with females was all that I knew. I never imagined sex with a male. Sure, I had noticed or envied guys with great bodies while playing high school football, but I never thought of it in a sexual context. I had never before given a man's body

such lofty regard as I did with Kelvin. How would I have known that rubbing two male sexual organs together would bring such a complete feeling of ecstasy? (17)

Raymond's reflection conveys surprise as much as it does pleasure. This is quickly followed by guilt and fear about what it would mean if his sexual relationship with Kelvin were revealed. Worrying that Kelvin might tell other people about the tryst, Raymond considers dropping out of school and thinks about "the humiliation [his] parents and fraternity would feel" (19).

> I often wondered why this [sexual relationship with Kelvin] had happened to me. Would this relationship and the new revelations I experienced with Kelvin change the carefully laid plans that my parents and Sela had mapped out for my future? How would I make room in my life for this? (30)

Before becoming sexually involved with Kelvin, Raymond describes his plans for a respectable life as his own. Here, there is a subtle but profound shift when he refers to "the carefully laid plans that [his] parents and Sela had mapped out." Because he feels such strong desire for Kelvin and perceives his relationship with Kelvin as incompatible with economic success and heterosexual, monogamous marriage, Raymond starts to experience the respectable life as something imposed from outside by others.

Not knowing how to deal with the conflict, Raymond seeks answers from Kelvin, who insists that no one needs to know and that he should maintain his relationship with Sela as if nothing has changed.

> My relationship with Sela remained the same. As far as she knew, Kelvin was no more than a face in the crowd. She was busy with [cheerleading] and her sorority. We continued to do things that we always shared. Our lovemaking was frequent and passionate, and when I experienced

difficulties getting in the mood, I would conjure up thoughts of my love-making sessions with Kelvin. It wasn't hurting anyone and Sela seemed satisfied. I assumed she was satisfied. I sometimes wondered if it wasn't an act. I mean, I had always heard all this stuff about women faking orgasms. At least with Kelvin and me the proof was there. He was a sexual cyclone. (30)

Again, Raymond draws a contrast between Sela and Kelvin and female and male sexuality. His uncertainty about Sela's orgasms is juxtaposed with how, with Kelvin, "the proof was there." The differences, however, do not erase or preclude his desire and love for Sela.

When Raymond considers his relationships with Kelvin and Sela, he feels a sense of closeness with Kelvin as a masculine black man and a desire for Sela as a feminine black woman.

Two able-bodied black men, in a town where most of its citizens were as white as the snow that now covered it, kissing like nothing else mattered but the moment. I looked up at the transparent sky and suddenly realized the importance of that moment; my lust for Kelvin had slowly turned to love. . . . There were times, however, when I needed Sela, not just for public appearances, but because deep in my heart I truly cared for her. Times when I only wanted to be wrapped in her small arms, lying there, looking at her, smelling her. I thought of the countless times I had told Sela I loved her and really meant it, but I couldn't understand why it was impossible to tell Kelvin just once. Was it possible to be in love with two people at the same time? (34)

It is their differences from each other that both attracts and confuses Raymond. There is something deeply satisfying about being "two able-bodied black men" surrounded by white people and loving each other. At the same time, he finds emotional and physical intimacy with Sela, something he can't "for some reason" have with Kelvin. In a world where one is either straight *or* gay, Raymond desires and loves both Kelvin and

Sela, and in a mononormative world, he wonders, is "it possible to be in love with two people at the same time?"

> Even though I had felt close to Kelvin, we never talked about gay things. It was always school, sports and girls. At first we were just two guys fucking; later, two men who loved each other and who enjoyed a sexual relationship. We played the same head trips with each other that occurred in male-female relationships and sought the same kind of security. Even though Kelvin and I shared a great many secrets, there was no one I could talk to about him. (49)

Raymond is sexually involved and in love with Kelvin, but there is nothing "gay" about their relationship. They continue to talk about "school, sports, and girls." They have an intimate relationship, but neither can reveal it to others for they both have too much to lose. They are, for all intents and purposes, "on the DL" and remain so until they both graduate and go their separate ways.

New York and "The Gay Lifestyle"

When Ray moves to New York for law school, finishes in the top half of his class, and is hired by "one of the top New York firms," his relationships with Sela and Kelvin become "things of the past" (36), and Raymond explores the possibility of identifying as gay rather than being on the DL.

> I had new friends, a new apartment and a new attitude about life. My life was totally different from the one I had lived down South. I no longer considered myself straight . . . but was I completely gay? (36)

For Raymond, being "completely gay" means adopting the identity and immersing himself into a gay community, both of which conflict with the sexual desire and emotional intimacy he experiences with women and his Southern roots and commitment to being respectable in the eyes of his family and community of origin. He is drawn, however, to being "completely gay" because it would mean that he is no longer on the DL.

The juxtaposition between being gay on the one hand and being on the DL on the other is embodied, respectively, by his best friend, Kyle, and Kelvin. While Christmas shopping in a New York department store, Raymond randomly runs into Kelvin. It has been six years since they last saw each other, and as they exchange greetings, a woman asks Kelvin to introduce her to Ray. The woman is Candance, Kelvin's fiancée. Raymond learns that their wedding day is the same as Ray's birthday, and Candance insists that Ray come to the wedding. "Married, I thought to myself, Kelvin, *married*? I chuckled out loud at the thought and wondered if his future wife knew what I knew" (42).

Later that evening, Ray is talking with his friend Kyle at a gay bar. "Kyle and I were both laughing out of control at my previous encounter with Kelvin and Candance" (43). Kyle says, "Chile, these confused boys give me fever. How long do you think that marriage is going to last before Mr. Kelvin starts sneaking out on Miss What's Her Name?" (43). Kyle is a self-identified gay, black man.

> Kyle appeared to be quite comfortable with who he was. A black man and gay. This sometimes made me a little bit uncomfortable. When I asked him how long he had been gay, he laughed, "Chile, I've been a sissy since I was in my mother's womb." (46)

Kyle is embedded in black gay culture in New York and proudly claims the identities "black man" and "gay," as well as "sissy," and indicates he was born that way. Kyle uses terms and language specific to black gay culture and does so with an exaggerated "finger snap or pop" (48). Kyle articulates the homonormative assertion that one is either gay or straight, and if you are having sex with both women and men, you must be one of those "confused boys."

Also in Kyle's statement about Kelvin is an assumption that Kelvin is closeted (which he is) and would have to "sneak out" on his wife—that is, "cheat" on her.

> Kyle quickly became my first openly gay friend. At times the relationship was trying, while at other times it was like a breath of fresh air in a smoke-filled room. . . . Sometimes [Kyle] would look at me in amazement at my naïveté about the gay life. It was completely different from the world I as used to. . . . Most of the time I felt as though I were in a different country, not really fitting in. But by now I didn't feel a part of the straight world either. My transition to the black gay community reminded me of high school . . . when I was one of twenty-two blacks in my freshman class of eight hundred forty-three. (48–49)

Raymond finds something that feels right in being himself around Kyle. "Kyle was the first person who I believed loved me no matter what. With Kyle, I became more comfortable with who I was and whom I had become" (50).

However, Raymond frequently reflects on how he does not quite fit in and how Kyle's life, especially the emphasis on sex rather than love, could never be satisfying to him.

> Somehow I managed not to become involved in this seedy side of the life, which . . . included gay bathhouses. I tried hard not to pass judgment on Kyle and others who chose that route. I learned not to be surprised at the number of professional black men who led secret lives. Had I stayed in Alabama, my life would have become similar. There was no way I would involve my family in my gay lifestyle. Besides, I came to realize that it was a lifestyle and not my life. (168)

Unlike Kyle, Raymond sees being gay as a lifestyle choice rather than his "life." This is grounded not in denial, but instead in a self-acceptance of his desire for love, intimacy, and commitment. In the New York gay world, men were either gay or on the DL, and in Alabama, men who love men have to be on the DL, none of which appeal to him.

It would be easy to see Raymond's discomfort as an unwillingness to accept his own homosexuality and a refusal to claim a gay identity. Certainly, this was the mainstream media narrative about African American MSWM. In one of the few academic analyses of *Invisible Life*, Lisa Jackson (2012) suggests that Raymond's refusal to accept his gay identity hinges on being black and the structural and cultural difficulties African Americans face when trying to achieve the American dream. She writes,

> While African Americans had made considerable strides in the area of equality by the 1990's, they were still struggling to prove themselves within the dominant culture; and it can be further extrapolated that for those male members who are homosexual, the American Dream continues to be just that—an elusive ideal that will not soon become their reality. (1096)

Jackson assumes that Raymond is homosexual and cannot admit or accept it. Discussing Raymond's expression of desire for both Kelvin and Sela, she writes, "The incongruence . . . is lost on Ray, probably because he is so busy walking the line that he cannot recognize that he has actually already crossed it, has already chosen a side" (1098). By suggesting that Raymond has already "chosen a side" by having sex with Kelvin, Jackson essentializes sexual identities as an expression of inherent desires and a fixed homosexual *or* heterosexual self.

While I agree with Jackson's assertion that the politics of respectability and structural barriers to the American dream are central to Raymond's struggle, I disagree that, for Raymond, it manifests as a denial of his homosexuality. First, Raymond never claims the identity gay. When he uses a label to describe himself, it is usually "bisexual," though that label also does not sit quite right with him. The first time he meets Janelle (JJ), his other close friend in New York, she propositions him by saying, "Every man I meet these days wants to get in my pants, Raymond, but to be honest with you, I wouldn't mind if you wanted to too" (52). Raymond replies, "I'm sure that would be nice, but uh . . . uh, Janelle, I'm gay or I guess you could say bisexual" (52). Second, Ray consistently talks about sex with women as pleasurable, and more important for my purposes, he falls in love with women and men simultaneously. Although he continuously questions it, he can love more than one person at the same time.

Raymond is caught in a liminal space between the gay and straight world, New York and Alabama, and it is this liminality that opens him to the desire to have more than one partner. If we consider the possibility that Raymond is not homosexual, and instead bisexual and *polyqueer*, it becomes clear that the compulsory and mononormative requirement to choose one person is the problem. This becomes undeniable when Quinn, a married black man on the DL, and Nicole, the woman he wants to marry, come into the narrative.

Quinn and Nicole

Raymond meets Quinn one night in a gay bar. Raymond is strongly attracted to Quinn, and with some prodding from his friends, decides to leave the bar with him. Upon learning that Quinn is planning to get a hotel room for the night, Ray invites him to sleep on his pullout couch. In the taxi, Raymond notices that Quinn is wearing "gold cuff links on his white French cuffs and what appeared to be a stainless steel Rolex" (62). After wondering for a moment whether or not it was real, Raymond concludes that it is because of "the way Quinn was dressed and his nice leather Hartmann briefcase" (62). Quinn's class status indicates that he is respectable, and as a gay black man as well, he brings together two seemingly incompatible worlds for Raymond.

Not only is Quinn upper class, handsome, and gay, he is also open to emotional as well as sexual intimacy. "Quinn's first kiss was gentle," and after they fall on to Ray's bed, Quinn pulls away and says, "Let's just lie here and talk. I could just look into those beautiful eyes of yours for the rest of my life. Maybe I'll discover what's going on behind them" (69). When the topic of other lovers comes up and Ray says, "Maybe you have a lover," Quinn responds, "No, I don't have a lover. What about you?" Ray says, "No way. I'm too independent and gay relationships just don't last" (69). They have a discussion about "protection" and whether or not they've each been tested for HIV—both have and were negative.

Without having sex, Quinn falls asleep during their conversation. Ray gets up to check his locks and change the music to Whitney Houston; he reflects, "For some strange reason Whitney always brought Kelvin to mind, but not tonight" (70). When he returns to bed, Quinn pulls Ray into his arms and holds him. "Maybe this is the one, I thought to myself. He's tall, black, handsome and smart" (71). The contrast between Quinn and Kelvin is striking. Unlike Kelvin on the DL, Quinn appears to be a respectable gay black man and perhaps "the one" who will give Raymond everything he desires.

The next day, Raymond returns to Birmingham to spend Christmas with his family. He reflects upon the internal conflict he feels about his sexual orientation and his relationship with his parents, especially his father, who was "the last of a dying breed. A strong, confident, self-made, proud black man" (88). Though his parents know about Raymond's "lifestyle" (83), neither had ever spoken about it. When his mother tells him that she will be proud of him no matter the "choices" he makes, Ray says, "I didn't have the heart to tell her that there were some things you didn't have a choice about. . . . No black man in his right mind would choose to be gay" (84). Because of Raymond's lifestyle, his relationship with his father is cold and distant. "I knew Pops would take my new sexual orientation as a personal slap in the face against him. That it would cause him a great deal of pain and concern. Not to mention his anger" (88).

The juxtaposition of Quinn, Ray's new lover in New York and possibly "the one," and his family in Birmingham punctuates the conflict Ray feels about having desire for men and being a respectable black man like his Pops. Ray's "new sexual orientation" creates a rift and distance from his Birmingham roots, but at the same time, Quinn is a successful black man in his own right and therefore might bridge the gap.

Christmas night, when Ray retires to his childhood bedroom, he checks his home answering machine. There are four messages from Quinn. While Ray listens to them, a commercial featuring Bo Jackson comes on the television.

> As I listened to Quinn's eloquent deep voice and watched Bo Jackson's perfect body, I realized that I had developed a noticeable erection in my pants. . . . I reached into my pants and removed my penis, placed it into the palm of my hand and beat myself into a guilty pleasure. Relieved, I looked up at the ceiling of this room where I had spent so many nights doing the exact same thing. Only then the pictures in my mind were of Sela or Janet Jackson. *How times had changed.* (92; italics in original)

At this point in the narrative, it appears that Raymond is gay and, perhaps, he and Quinn can be two respectable gay black men together.

However, as is the case throughout the novel, a possible resolution to Raymond's dilemma is confounded by his desire for women. While still in Birmingham, Raymond sets up a meeting to see Sela. On his way to meet her, Raymond runs into Margo, a girl from high school with whom he had his first sexual experience. Margo "played an important part in my sexual development," having been "the first girl, or the first person for that matter, to give me head" (95). While talking with Margo, Ray "realized that it was another secret I had kept from Sela and my parents too" (96). Though subtle, this thought reveals a discomfort with sexual secrets in general, not just those he keeps about his sexual relationships with men.

After a brief exchange about Raymond's success as a litigation attorney and that he is no longer with Sela, they say their goodbyes. "Margo reached up and gave me a big hug and gently bit the end of my ear, which caused a nice tingling sensation. Well, I guess I still have it, I thought to myself" (96). Sela arrives, and after catching up on each other's lives, including that Sela is engaged, they end up in bed together. There is no doubt that Raymond is aroused and enjoys having sex with Sela.

> All the years we had dated and all the times we had made love could not measure up with what was occurring in this hotel suite. My sex ached with such power that I could feel it growing harder and longer. (108)

When Sela asks him if he has protection, and Ray says that he'll withdraw before he ejaculates, Sela says that she wants to, but "no." Sela flips Ray over on to his back.

> Starting with my toes, she used her tiny tongue and licked my entire body, lingering at my sex. I gazed around the room in total shock and complete ecstasy. It felt wonderful. Sela attacked oral sex with great intensity. This was the first time she had ever done anything remotely close to this. Where did she learn this, I wondered in my enjoyment? (109)

Raymond is so aroused by this that he once again prepares to enter Sela. As he does so, he thinks about his "past sexual partners," and refuses to "risk endangering Sela" (107). With this thought, he loses his erection. It is not sex with a woman that turns Raymond off; it is the thought of putting Sela at risk of HIV infection. Moreover, when she compliments him on his lovemaking skills, Raymond wonders, "Had sleeping with men made me a better lover with women?" (109). This is not the internal dialogue of a closeted gay man. There is something decidedly queer about Raymond's desire, not just because he experiences sexual pleasure with women and men, but also because he contemplates how sex with men complements rather than contradicts having sex with women.

Despite the pleasure he experiences with Sela and his curiosity about how being bisexual might make him a better lover, he once again struggles with the voice of homonormativity—the voice that comes from his life in New York and that makes his embodied desire dissonant with an intelligible sexual identity.

I . . . asked myself why this had happened. What was I trying to prove? A couple of nights ago I was in heat over Bo Jackson and Quinn. Tonight I was in bed with an almost married woman. I thought it was time for me to return to New York before I ruined other people's lives as I had ruined my own. I knew that this night would not change me the way the night in my apartment with Kelvin had so many years ago. I tried to determine the difference between making love with a woman and with a man. While I had enjoyed this night of passion with Sela, I wondered if I had been too methodical in my lovemaking or if I had allowed myself to just let go as I had done so many time before with male partners. Was making love to a woman now work instead of enjoyment for me? (110)

In this passage, Raymond does not conclude that he is gay. Instead, he asks hard questions and wonders whether or not making love with Sela was an attempt to prove to himself that he is not gay—a common, homonormative discourse about ostensibly bisexual men sleeping with women to deny their "true" identity. He did not feel the same passion as he does with his male partners, but he enjoyed having sex with Sela. He lost his erection only when he recognized how he had been dishonest with her. In the end, the combination of his own dishonesty, Sela's cheating on her fiancé, and the passion he feels for men pull him toward New York and his gay "lifestyle" and away from his life in Birmingham, embodied by Sela and reflected in the respectable life of his parents.

As they are about to say their goodbyes, Sela says that Raymond changed when he went to New York and that she had always dreamed of marrying him. Ray says, "I never stopped loving you. But I want you to be happy and I'm not certain that I can give you what you deserve. . . . Someone who worships the ground you walk on. Someone who loves you more than you love him" (112). Raymond's doubts about being able to love Sela the way she deserves come from the mononormative assumption that one person should fulfill every need. Raymond doesn't feel the sexual passion with women he feels with men, but there is no doubt that he is sexually attracted to and loves women. Upon parting,

Raymond reflects, "The time we had spent together would always be special to me and I would never forget her. . . . As I kissed Sela . . . everything was . . . as it had always been . . . the same, and yet it was so very different" (113).

When Raymond returns to New York, he finds a gold wedding band in his apartment. Realizing it is Quinn's, Ray is once again faced with being involved with a man on the DL. While holding the ring in his hand, his phone rings. It is Candance, Kelvin's fiancée, calling to invite him to a concert with her, Kelvin, and her best friend, Nicole. Ray agrees, and upon meeting Nicole is struck by her class, beauty, and poise and learns that she is a talented stage actress. The compulsory need to choose between being gay or being a respectable black man intensifies when Nicole comes into Raymond's life. Just as was the case with Sela and Kelvin, Nicole and Quinn represent the respectable life of middle-class heteronormativity and the DL.

Quinn begs Ray for forgiveness for not telling him that he is married to a woman and requests that they "start all over as friends" (130). Raymond acquiesces and after they make love, "tenderly attending to each other's needs," Quinn wishes "that life could be like this forever." They spend several days together in Ray's apartment getting to know each other better and falling in love. After those days of having sex, talking, ordering take out, and drinking Champagne and chardonnay, they "decided to take a break from each other" (133).

> When Quinn left, I felt brand-new. I was able to put my problems in proper perspective. I was ready to take on the world, or at least New York City. (133)

Here, Raymond feels "brand-new" because, despite Quinn being on the DL, he fulfills Raymond's emotional and physical needs, and Raymond is poised to accept his gay "lifestyle." While he is ready to "at least" take on New York, his ability to take on "the world" once again is confounded by his love and desire for a woman.

While taking the break from Quinn, Ray is invited by Nicole to a performance of *Dreamgirls* in which she will be playing one of the lead roles.

> Minutes into the show Nicole Springer had won me over. . . . I watched Nicole's every move onstage. When she wasn't onstage, I waited with excitement for her return. I hardly noticed all the good-looking men in the cast. Besides, I had seen many of them in the bars. (139)

As Ray begins to get to know her, he realizes that she is the perfect respectable woman.

> Not only was she beautiful, she was extremely smart. . . . She was truly a Southern belle, a new type of belle but a belle nonetheless. She had a certain sex appeal that was hard to ignore, a quiet confidence in the way she carried herself that no man in his right mind could resist. (142)

Nicole invites Raymond to attend church with her and later reveals that she will not have sex with a man until she knows the relationship will lead to marriage.

When Nicole tells Ray, "All the men I meet are one of three things: white, married or gay" (143), Raymond is once again confronted with questions about his own identity, desires, and relationships, but now those questions revolve around the infidelity and dishonesty that comes with being on the DL.

> As Nicole talked, I thought to myself how tough it must be for black women these days. I mean, being black and gay was tough enough, but I had never stopped to think how difficult it must be for sharp black women. Maybe that was why she hadn't asked me the gay question. Did she know and just want a new friend or did she really think that I was straight? Or was she willing to take me in my present condition? (143)

Reflecting on how difficult it is for talented, smart, beautiful black women to find respectable partners, Raymond wonders if her limited choices might allow her to open up to him in his "present condition." Here we see the first glimpse of Raymond's hopefulness about being accepted as "not completely gay, but not straight either." When talking with JJ and Kyle about Nicole, Ray says, "She's nice and very special. But I'm not about to change my religion" (154).

However, as time passes, he falls in love with Nicole while still being in love with Quinn. When a client and man on the DL, NFL star Basil Henderson, propositions Raymond, he responds by saying, "I'm seeing someone" (167). Proud of having turned down Basil, Ray remarks, "I smiled to myself at how easily 'I'm seeing someone' fell from my lips. Whom was I talking about, Quinn or Nicole?" (167).

After leaving Basil, Ray meets Kyle at the gay bar and expresses concern over Kyle's joblessness and promiscuity. Taking a walk to clear his head, Ray's thoughts turn to HIV and how it was "hitting the black gay community with devastating force, and with all the closeted black men out there like Basil, it would soon hit the heterosexual community with equal force" (171).

Attaching the threat of HIV to men on the DL, Raymond wants to do things differently. He returns to his apartment to find a dozen roses from Quinn and a potted plant from Nicole. Both have written affectionate cards, and after reading them, Ray is ecstatic. "My mood abruptly switched from a depressed state to one of complete euphoria. It couldn't get much better than this" (172). In love with and loved by both Quinn and Nicole, Raymond is deeply satisfied. "My life was changing and I couldn't ever remember being this happy as an adult" (174). As he thinks about Quinn and Nicole, he is struck by how complementary they are in their fulfillment of different needs.

The first time I kissed [Nicole] in a romantic way, I felt as though I was tasting heat. Her body was so warm that it oozed a sexual mist. When our foreplay reached the danger zone, Nicole pulled back and explained that she wasn't a virgin, but that the next time she went all the way, it would be for love. I, of course, was very understanding, and in many ways it relieved a lot of pressure that was building within me. (173)

Raymond is relieved that Nicole does not want to go "all the way," and certainly this could reflect an exclusively homoerotic orientation. However, he has strong sexual desire for Nicole—though perhaps not as strong as his desire for Quinn, and the meaning of "pressure" is left ambiguous. Is it a pressure to perform sexually without desire *or*, given his sexually intimate love affair with Quinn, is it pressure to have sex with Nicole and once again be on the DL? This passage continues,

Quinn was still very much in the picture and he more than adequately took care of my sexual needs; in fact, he met both my physical and emotional needs without complications. . . . I had only casually mentioned Nicole, so he assumed he was the only reason I appeared to be floating among the stars. . . . The truth of the matter was that the combination of the two had sent me into orbit. (173–174)

Here, it is not a secret desire for men, but instead, his desire for a woman that places Raymond on the DL, an outcome resulting from a homonormative insistence on being "completely gay" and monogamous with Quinn. Despite having chosen a gay lifestyle, Raymond's satisfaction is found in "the combination of the two." In Raymond's desire, Nicole and Quinn are not in opposition to each other, as was the case with Kelvin and Sela. Instead, they are complementary and send him "into orbit."

Susan [Ray's colleague] helped me pick out some diamond stud earrings for Nicole's Valentine's present. Kyle helped pick out sexy underwear for Quinn. . . . My life was changing and I couldn't ever remember being this happy. (174)

While watching the Spike Lee film *Mo' Better Blues* with Nicole, Ray straightforwardly states that he wants both Nicole and Quinn.

> We popped corn, drank white wine and watched the movie. It played like a movie of my present life, with the lead character trying to make a choice. My situation was a little different, since Denzel was choosing between two women and I was going to have to make a choice between a man and a woman. For the first time I realized I wanted them both. (180)

Raymond is on the DL with both Nicole and Quinn, not because he is gay, but instead, because he is *polyamorous* in a mononormative world. That is, he loves and desires Nicole and Quinn, and significantly, he wants them *both* while the gay and straight worlds demand that he choose one *or* the other. Here we see an aspect of Raymond's sexual orientation that is unintelligible in heteronormative *and* homonormative narratives about the "black man on the down low." In wanting both and seeing them as complimentary, not contradictory, Raymond confounds the heternormative *and* homonormative insistence on being *monogamous*.

Not only does mononormativity preclude his ability to have both, it also renders his bisexual desires invisible.

> Being gay was such a small part of who I was. Maybe keeping my gayness a secret was creating the low self-esteem. But was I gay or bisexual and what was the difference? Many gay men viewed bisexuality with misgivings. The feeling was that bisexuality was a cop-out. That you were one or the other, no in-between. Did I hang on to my bisexuality because it was more acceptable? The bottom line was how I felt about the people I was involved with. I wouldn't allow society's labels to run my life. (206)

Here he moves from "gayness" to questioning whether he is gay or bisexual until finally he concludes that the labels don't fit given how he "felt about the people" he loves. This is a *polyqueer* turn in his self-understanding. Rather than taking on a label that restricts his love to men or women, he will "run his life" based on the love he feels for two people and, in his insistence on plurality, queers sexual orientation.

Not only does Raymond's polyqueer orientation confound notions of sexual identity, there are indications that it changes his masculinity, not by making him "sissy" or effeminate, but instead, by instilling a certain feminist awareness and sensibility in relationships to women.

> I realized how much Candance and Nicole were alike: aggressive yet feminine, the complete embodiment of the perfect woman. They both were sophisticated but possessed unpretentious qualities that I had always admired in my mother. . . . Like Nicole, she was as smart as she was beautiful. What was it about women like Nicole and Candance and bisexual men? Was it because many of us were very bright and good-looking? Were we more sensitive than heterosexual men? What was it about these women that caused gay and bisexual men to forget about their secret sexual desires? I asked myself the questions, but I didn't have the answers. (186)

In addition to thinking perhaps he was a better lover with Sela because he had sex with men, Raymond suggests there might be an affinity between "sensitive" bisexual men and strong, confident black women. He wonders why strong, confident women are drawn to "bisexual men" and why these women can make "gay and bisexual men . . . forget about their secret sexual desires."

Unlike Raymond, I wonder less about an affinity between strong, confident women and bisexual men (a topic I will take up in more detail later), and instead question why bisexual men have to "forget about their secret sexual desires" in order to be with women. The night that Raymond tells Nicole that he is in love with her, they "went further than we ever had without actual penetration."

> I had become pretty good at pleasing women with oral sex. . . . Nicole's own expertise was a revelation. I found it interesting that oral sex was no

longer taboo in the black community, as it once had been. I wondered if the taboo against homosexuals would eventually die. There was a time when black men never admitted to oral sex, but now they bragged about it. It was thought that only weak men or sissies would participate in such an act. (211)

After revealing that he is "pretty good" at cunnilingus and that receiving oral sex from Nicole was a "revelation," Raymond draws a connection between his homoerotic desire for men and performing oral sex on women. If norms around oral sex could change, perhaps so could attitudes about homoerotic desire. Raymond is well aware that his life would be very different if being a respectable and masculine black man did not exclude having sexual and romantic relationships with men. More important for Raymond, however, is an acceptance of not just homoerotic desire, but also non-monogamy. Because he has sexual desire for and is in love *with two people*—a man and a woman—and he wants them both, social acceptance of homoerotic desire would not be enough to solve his dilemma. The taboo against non-monogamy and loving more than one person would also have to change, not just in the minds of "the black community," but also in the minds of the women who are partnered with men like Raymond.[5]

Raymond's choices are constrained by compulsory monogamy, not an internal, fixed desire for men *or* for women. At one point, Kelvin suggests that Raymond marry Nicole so that Ray and Kelvin can "be together forever." In Raymond's mononormative world, he is "appalled" by the suggestion because it is not "fair to Nicole and Candance." Kelvin responds, "It's not hurting anyone, especially if they're happy." To this, Raymond says, "I haven't made the choices about my life that you have. I don't know if I'm going to end up with a man or a woman. To be honest with you, I'm appalled at your suggestions" (190). The unintelligibility of polyamory, as well as a heterosexist conflation of homoerotic desire with inferiority, would force Raymond and Kelvin to keep their love a secret. In a *polyqueer* world where homoerotic desire is not contradictory to being a respectable black man *and* where polyamory is a viable option, Raymond and Kelvin could be open and honest with Candance and Nicole, allowing them to consciously choose whether or not they want to be partnered with Kelvin and Raymond.

Alas, Raymond's desire to have both Quinn and Nicole is impossible to fulfill in a world that demands monogamy. The necessity to choose, like the pressure to become a particular kind of respectable black man, comes from the outside world, this time from his friends in New York. In a conversation with JJ about Nicole, Raymond does not want to choose one over the other, but JJ insists he must.

> RAYMOND: I . . . want to start out right. I mean, I could marry this girl.
>
> JJ: But why, Ray? Are you being true to yourself? I know you don't like to admit it, but Quinn makes you happy.
>
> RAYMOND: So does Nicole.
>
> JJ: But you haven't even had sex with her.
>
> RAYMOND: How do you know that?'
>
> JJ: Trust me, you would have said something.
>
> RAYMOND: But I am sexually attracted to her.
>
> JJ: That's because she's an unattainable beauty queen. The movie star type.
>
>   How are you going to feel when she grows old or when you see another fine man like Quinn or that Steve-Basil guy?
>
> RAYMOND: You don't understand. . . . Nicole does things for me that no person has ever done. She makes me feel like I could run the world if I wanted to. I'm tired of worrying if somebody is really faithful. I want somebody who may love me more than I love them.
>
> JJ: But is that fair to Nicole or are you being selfish?
>
> RAYMOND: JJ, with Nicole I think I could give up the life. I like her as a person. I want to take care of her. I want to grow old with her.
>
> JJ: Are you sure you're not doing this for your parents?
>
> RAYMOND: No.[6]
>
> JJ: So you're not gay anymore?

RAYMOND: You know that I'm not totally gay. . . . JJ, I'll always have
   desires for men. But I'll just suppress them.
JJ: For how long?
RAYMOND: As long as I'm in love with Nicole.
JJ: Well, baby, you know I wish you well. What I think you should have
   done is made Quinn yours completely. I'm not certain I believe
   totally in this bisexual thing. (222–223)

If compulsory monogamy did not force Raymond to choose, he would
not have to suppress his desire for men or give up Quinn in order to be
with Nicole.

Reflecting on his conversation with JJ, Raymond feels hopeful,
not about having both, but instead about his ability to be with just
Nicole.

My conversation and brunch with JJ gave me a lot to think about. I trea-
sured her comments, but only I knew how I felt inside. Nicole made me
feel like I had butterflies in my stomach. When I was with her, I didn't
think about men. I was not going to give up on the dream of being totally
happy with just one person, one woman, no matter what JJ thought. Another man would never be able to give me that. That part of my life would
just have to remain invisible. (224)

Raymond wants to be in an intimate and sexual relationship with both.
Nicole fulfills some needs, while Quinn fulfills others. The only reason
he is "not going to give up on the dream of being totally happy with
just one person, one woman" is not because that is what he wants. It
is because that is what his parents and friends want. "I had come to
the conclusion that I was passionately attracted to women and sexually
attracted to men" (211). But what if he didn't have to choose? What if
Raymond could be with Nicole *and* Quinn?

When Candance, Kelvin's fiancée, is diagnosed with AIDS, Raymond
decides that he must be honest with Nicole.

RAYMOND: I'm gay, Nicole . . . well, I guess you could say I'm
bisexual . . .

NICOLE: You're kidding . . . right? . . .

RAYMOND: I'm sorry, Nicole. I know I should have said something
earlier.

NICOLE: Sorry? . . . Sorry, after you made love to me less than a week
ago? Why me, Raymond?

RAYMOND: Because I love you.

NICOLE: Love me? How can you love me? You love men . . . isn't that
what you're telling me? . . . You lied to me Raymond. I can't forgive
that.

RAYMOND: I didn't lie, Nicole. Maybe I just didn't tell the whole
truth. . . . Nicole, I didn't mean to fall in love with you. . . . And when
I did, I was going to tell you. I do love you . . .

NICOLE: Right now I don't have time to talk. . . . Right now my best
friend is down the hallway, fighting for her life. Probably because of
loving someone like you . . . (237)

Nicole asks, "How can you love me? You love men." This is certainly
an insistence on being either gay or straight and erases bisexuality,
but it also reflects an underlying assumption that it is possible to
love only one person. Even with this, Nicole says, "I don't doubt that
you love me, Raymond. Of that I am sure. I mean, I have to believe
that you love me. But do you love me enough?" She is asking if he
loves her enough to give up men. When Raymond answers, "I think
so." She says, "[T]hat's not good enough. I can't base my future on
an 'I think so'" (237). While possible exposure to HIV is a significant
motivation for her rejection, she is clear that his dishonesty and the
prospect of ongoing infidelity are far more painful and unacceptable.
In a mononormative world, she expects and wants monogamy and
cannot trust Raymond to give up sex with men for the rest of their
lives together.

After this rejection, Raymond falls into a tailspin of depression and drinking. When his father shows up in New York to make sure he is okay, Raymond tells him the truth as well.

> Pops, no matter what you think of me, I'm no sissy. I am the man you raised me to be. My gayness is such a small part of who I've become. Look around you, Pops. I've accomplished a lot in my life. I am making a contribution. I've earned your respect, Pops. . . . [I]t was just something I discovered about myself later in life. Something that brought pleasure to my body. I'm very much a man. I have never had a desire to be anything else. You have succeeded in what you set out to do. I am a proud black man who loves women, but I have loved men too, Pops. (245–246)

Raymond refuses to be defined by his sexual orientation and rejects the notion that a respectable, proud black man can't love women and men.

After reconciling with his father, Raymond writes Nicole a long letter. In it, he offers a utopian vision of a world in which he and Nicole can be honest with each other.

> *In a perfect world we would accept people for who and what they are. No strings, complete honesty, total acceptance, no matter what. In this imperfect world we live in, there is no longer dignity in telling the truth. . . . I wanted our relationship to be unique. Totally honest. There are countless thousands of women out there today in love with bisexual men, without their knowledge. This side of me is such a small part of who I am. Would you please look further into who I am totally? . . . If we shared a life together, I would be true to our relationship, no matter what my desires dictated. In a perfect world that would be enough. That love will keep me faithful to you and our future. . . . I ask you for forgiveness. Not for my sexual orientation but because I didn't tell you up front.* (250; italics in original)

In this letter, Raymond refers to a "unique" relationship in which he could be honest about who is and not be reduced to his sexual orientation. He finally accepts his desire for men and women and asks Nicole to do the same. With this huge step in his own consciousness, he moves forward on a path that is respectable, but also neither heterosexual or homosexual. And yet Raymond still holds on to the idea of monogamy, hoping "that love will keep me faithful to you and our future."

The novel ends with a phone conversation between Nicole and Raymond. She is calling to wish him happy birthday and to request his presence at her opening night on Broadway. At the end of the conversation, Nicole asks, "Raymond, can I ask you one more thing? . . . When do you stop wishing for something that may never happen? When do you stop wishing for that perfect world?" (265). To this, Raymond responds, "Never . . . Nicole . . . never" (265).

As a black man who has desire for women and men, loves two people, and wants them both, Raymond Tyler Jr. lives an invisible life. His life is invisible because his desire for women and men *and his desire to not have to choose between two people he loves* are unintelligible. Rather than a duplicitous decision to deceive the people in his life, Raymond is on the DL because he understands that, in this world, he will lose not only respectability, but also the intimate, loving relationships for which he so longs.

While the title of the novel initially signifies the secret of Raymond's relationships with men, in the end, the invisibility is the unintelligibility of *polyamory* and his desire to love black women and black men. The entire narrative revolves around Raymond's wish that he could just choose to be gay or to be straight and be faithful to his partner, whoever it would be. However, that wish does not reflect his sexual *and relationship* orientation as a black man. His struggle is with contorting himself into a world that demands one is either gay or straight and monogamous, none of which reflect his feelings, desires, and relationships. In the end, Raymond says he will never stop dreaming, not of being gay or straight himself, but instead of a "perfect world" in which he wouldn't have to choose and could be understood and loved by both Nicole and Quinn.

If we assume that Raymond is gay and simply cannot accept it, Sela and Nicole could be easily read as peripheral characters that stand in for the politics of respectability and as heteronormative obstacles to Raymond's acceptance of a true self and a homosexual identity. This reading, however, renders Sela and Nicole as signifiers for heternormative respectability rather than as full characters that represent black women and black female sexuality. Reading the text in this way reduces Sela and Nicole to their gender position and does not take into consideration race and the relationships between and among African American women and men.

Building on Michelle Wallace's use of the astrophysical metaphor of a black hole to discuss the invisibility of black creativity, Evelyn Hammonds (1997) suggests that the metaphor might also work well to make visible black female sexualities. Hammonds explains, "the observer outside of the (black) hole sees it as a void, an empty place in space. However, it is not empty; it is a dense and full place in space. . . . [W]e can detect the presence of a black hole by its effects on the region of space where it is located. . . . In the case of black female sexualities, this implies that we need to develop reading strategies that allow us to make visible the distorting and productive effects these sexualities produce in relation to more visible sexualities" (134–135).

Through the lens of Hammond's black hole metaphor, Sela and Nicole are not empty signifiers of Raymond's nonexistent heterosexuality. Instead, they have substance and represent a force that pulls Raymond, not toward heterosexuality, but toward them *as black women*. Though they are "invisible" when viewed through the homonormative lens of white sexualities, E. Lynn Harris writes Sela and Nicole as having "distorting and producing effects" on Raymond's dream of a perfect world.

Discussing the relationship between Shug and Celie in Alice Walker's *The Color Purple*, Hammonds says, "Rather than assuming that black female sexualities are structured along an axis of normal and perverse paralleling that of white women, we might find that for black women a different geometry operates. For example, acknowledging this difference I could read the relationship between Shug and Celie . . . as one that depicts desire between women and desire between women and men simultaneously, in dynamic relationship rather than in opposition" (135).

Raymond's love for Sela and Nicole is perhaps different from his love of Kelvin and Quinn, but is no less significant or "real." According to Hammonds, the geometry of black female sexualities includes "a polymorphous erotic that does not exclude desire for men but also does not privilege it" (135). Perhaps then, through a *polyquare*[7] (Johnson 2001) lens we can read Raymond's desire for women as consistent with rather than contradictory to his desire for men, and do so without privileging heterosexuality or homosexuality.

Conclusion

In this polyqueer reading of *Invisible Life*, the "perfect world" Raymond dreams of is one in which African American men could be contemporaneously sexually involved with and love women and men. It points to the ways in which mononormativity cuts across both black respectability and homonormativity and, within these constraints, how it is unacceptable to have two (or more) partners, especially if those partners are a man and a woman. The secret for Raymond Tyler is less about heterosexism, although that is part of his dilemma. He struggles less with his desire for both Quinn and Nicole and more with the requirement to *choose* between them and adopt an entire life. The secret that eats away at him is infidelity—being in love with two people and being dishonest about it. However, it is key that his dishonesty does not reflect a character flaw; it reflects a refusal to give up on the life he wants in order to conform to mononormative world in which "real men" are either respectable or gay. It is the intersection of mononormativity and the structural, cultural, and interpersonal prejudices and biases around race, sexuality, and gender that force Raymond into secrecy.

With a focus on not just heterosexism, but also mononormativity, we can see the DL as a *switchpoint* between the politics of black respectability and the homonormativity of the "gay lifestyle." Here I am relying on Kathryn Bond Stockton's (2007) method for examining the relationship between signifiers of "queer" and "black." According to Stockton, a switchpoint is "a point of connection between two signs (or two rather separate connotative fields) where something from one flows toward (is diverted in the direction of) the other, lending its connotative spread and signifying force to the other, illuminating it and intensifying it, but also sometimes shifting it or adulterating it" (5). Stockton suggests that switchpoints offer insight into the intersection of racial formation and queer politics that otherwise would not be visible.

The DL, as a switchpoint or hinge, connects "queer" and "black"—a point of intersection where black respectability and the whiteness of homonormativity flow into each other as compulsory monogamy. The requirements to choose either Sela *or* Kelvin, Nicole *or* Quinn, men *or* women, being a respectable black man *or* being a gay man are grounded in compulsory monogamy as much as race and sexual identity politics. Mononormativity is the switchpoint that splits the track into two and only two options and forces young men of color, if not onto one track or the other, then into secrecy to avoid the loss that would ensue by having to choose between being gay or black. In other words, while heteronormativity pulls Raymond toward black respectability and homonormativity insists that he "come out" as a gay man, compulsory monogamy forces Raymond into the secrecy of the DL and renders invisible his love of black women and black men, and his desire for polyamory.

3

Between (Polyamorous) Men

Polyqueer Homosocial Bonds in The Other Man

In her book *Between Men: English Literature and Male Homosocial Desire*, Eve Sedgwick (1985) explores the structure of men's relationships with other men in literature from the mid-eighteenth to the mid-nineteenth century. Her theoretical project is to identify how representations of sexuality signify power relations between women and men and among men. To illustrate this, she follows the historical trajectory of the literary construction of men's relationships with each other to define and identify what she refers to as *homosocial desire* between men. For Sedgwick, homosocial desire is the "affective or social force, the glue, even when its manifestation is hostility or hatred or something less emotively charged" that binds men to each other (2). She argues that changes in the structure of homosocial desire between men, including "male friendship, mentorship, entitlement, rivalry, and hetero- and homosexuality was in an intimate and shifting relation to class; and that no element of that pattern can be understood outside of this relation to women and the gender system as a whole" (1).

According to Sedgwick, homosocial bonds between men are often narrated as markers of class difference or sameness, but they are intelligible as distinct from men's relationships with women only through the erasure and/or disavowal of homosexual desire. This process, Sedgwick argues, hinges on the displacement of homosexual desire between men through narrative triangulation, specifically the replacement of homoerotic desires between men with competition for and rivalries over the same prized feminine sexual object. The presence of the woman as the object of exchange heterosexualizes the men's bond with each other, because the specter of homoerotic desire for each other is sublimated and displaced on to the woman. As long as they share a desire for her and not for each other, the WMM triangle ensures homosocial bonds between men are devoid of homoeroticism and distinct from homosexuality. Bonding as equals is left to the heterosexual men while erotic desire and sex is relegated to the bodies of women. Because the woman functions solely as the object of exchange between men, the love triangle situates the men as active subjects and the woman as the object of transaction, thereby reproducing heteronormative gender hierarchies. Because homosocial bonds between men depend upon WMM triangulation to secure heteromasculine domininance in relationship to not just women, but also homosexual men, the WMM love triangle and disavowal of homoerotic desire are important to feminist analysis.

My objective in this chapter is to offer a polyqueer reading of a narrative of competitive triangulation that is resolved not when the best man wins the girl, but instead when the men accept the woman's desire to have both of them. I ask, what happens to homosocial bonds between men and the relationship between masculine subjectivity and feminine objectification when, in the narrative, the men accept polyamory rather than eliminate the rival? What if the woman, rather than the men, is narrated as the desiring subject in erotic triangulation? Do narratives of consensual, polyamorous triangulation offer the potential to queer homosocial bonds between men and, by doing so, signify a feminist disruption in gendered power relations?

To explore and illustrate the feminist potential of polyqueer homosocial bonding, I will analyze the film *The Other Man* (2008) as a text that is less a critique of mononormativity, as was the case with E. Lynn Harris's *Invisible Life*, and more a narrative of competitive homosocial bonding that is resolved in *polyqueer homosociality*. By polyqueer homosociality, I mean bonds between men that result from a polyamorous resolution to WMM triangulation and that, through a poly resolution, reconfigure heteromasculinity in terms of its relationship to both the feminine sexual object and queer desire. Unlike homosocial bonds that straighten out men's relationships with each other through the objectification of women and disavowal of homoerotic desire, polyqueer homosocial bonds are formed when the men agree to accept the woman's desire for and relationship with the other.

The film is the story of a love triangle between a woman, Lisa, and two men, her husband, Peter, and her lover, Ralph. *The Other Man* is particularly interesting because the narrative begins with Peter and Ralph situated as rivals in competition for Lisa—Sedgwick's competitive triangle. Though Lisa begins as a sexual object and the medium of Peter and Ralph's relationship, by the end, she emerges as the sexual subject who brings the men together in relationship to each other in a queer sort of bonding and kinship. Unlike Sedgwick's love triangle, which involves two masculine subjects competing for a feminine sexual object, the polyamorous Vee in *The Other Man* places the woman's sexual subjectivity at the center, thereby necessitating a transformation of the men's masculinities and their relationship to each other.

Through this process, a queer bond emerges through triangulation, turning Sedgwick's homosociality on its head. This "insertion" of feminine sexual subjectivity into the relationship between the two men unravels the characters' masculinities and opens up an opportunity to transform their homosocial bond with each other. As I describe below, the resolution of the love triangle is not winner take all or reestablishment of a heteronormative, monogamous dyad, as Sedgwick would predict. Instead, the resolution is a polyqueer relationship between all of the characters that disrupts the dominance and superiority of heteromasculinity.

The Other Man as Rival

The film begins with a fashion show. Lisa, played by Laura Linney, is a shoe designer whose shoes are featured in the show. She is sitting with her husband, Peter, played by Liam Neeson and her adult daughter, Abigail, played by Romola Garai. As the camera focuses on Lisa, she looks off as if thinking about something else. Later, when Lisa and Peter are at dinner, she expresses some dissatisfaction over his attitude about her work as a shoe designer.

> LISA: I've got a daughter who flees and a husband who jeers.
> PETER: Oh, please. I don't jeer. I like your shoes. It's the people in them I can't stand.
> LISA: They make wonderful shoes.
> PETER: Hey. You make wonderful shoes.

Lisa's next line appears to be a shift in topic.

> LISA: Do you think two people can live together all their lives?
> PETER: We've managed more than half our lives. Do we have a problem?
> LISA: Of course we don't have a problem.
> PETER: Is that the problem? Heh? Why do you ask?

Lisa once again seems to shift the topic by bringing up their daughter's relationship with her boyfriend, George, played by Craig Parkinson. Peter expresses consternation over the relationship, and Lisa responds by asking if he is jealous of George. When he rejects the idea, Lisa says, "I think I like George," to which Peter responds, "Well, you have a strange taste in men." This strikes a chord with Lisa—seemingly distraught, she looks down. Clearly there is something more going on. She then looks up and says, "Do you never wish you might be given the chance to sleep with someone else?" When Peter asks, "Are you telling me something?" Lisa doesn't deny it, but says, "I'm asking." Peter replies, "No. I mean, No. I don't want to sleep with someone else. Maybe I haven't found the right person yet." Here again, Lisa looks off as if thinking about something or someone else. Resolved, Peter states unequivocally, "No. Never. I promise." Lisa abruptly looks up and says with equal conviction, "It's a choice, not a promise. You meet someone. You fall in love. You have the opportunity. You make a choice." When Peter says, "I chose you," Lisa smiles warmly and says, "I do love you, you know. You do know that, don't you? If I didn't, I'd go . . . just go. Taking nothing. Bare. Start again." The scene ends with Peter saying, "It's alright then." Lisa looks down again with sadness. Though she doesn't say it out loud, a voice in her head says, *I need to tell you something.*

In this exchange, we learn several things about Lisa and Peter's relationship. First, Lisa is less than satisfied with Peter's attitude about her work as a shoe designer. When Peter says, "You make wonderful shoes," Lisa immediately asks whether or not "two people can live together their entire lives." There is something about her family's dismissal of her work that is tied to her question about long-term relationships.

After wondering if people can live together their entire lives, Lisa brings up Abigail and the possibility of her marrying George. While this appears to be a change of subject, it links Lisa's skepticism toward long-term relationships with her daughter's future. Not only does this highlight the way in which monogamous marriage is the default and passed down through family, it also reveals that Lisa is ambivalent about marriage itself. She appears a bit hopeful about the prospect of Abigail marrying George, but at the same time, she is asking whether or not people can live together all their lives.

Peter also expresses some skepticism, but not toward the institution of marriage. Instead, he is skeptical of Abigail's choice of partner. When Lisa asks him if he is jealous, his response illuminates Peter's proprietary relationship to his daughter and raises the specter of male privilege in the form of ownership and exchange of women. By suggesting that his evaluation of George is relevant, Peter displaces Abigail's relationship with George with a relationship between himself and George. In other words, Peter situates himself as the proprietor of Abigail and is reluctant to enter in to an exchange relationship with George.

Finally, and most important, we learn in this scene that Lisa is having an affair. When Peter says, "[Y]ou have a strange taste in men," Lisa looks down, thinking of something or someone else and then immediately follows with a question about sexual fidelity. When Peter says that he has not "found the right person yet," Lisa again wistfully looks away, suggesting that perhaps she has. Peter says that he made "a promise" and she immediately replies, "It's a choice, not a promise. You meet someone. You fall in love. You have the opportunity. You make a choice." That she characterizes monogamy as a "choice" and juxtaposes this with Peter's "promise" renders *compulsory* monogamy suspect.

This contrast in perspective opens narrative space for consistency between Lisa's "choice" to have an affair on the one hand and remain with Peter on the other, a choice that will link Peter to the "other man." When Peter says that he chose her, Lisa explains that her love for Peter is what is keeping her in their marriage, and that she wants to be in a long-term committed relationship with him.

At the same time, it is clear that she is questioning monogamous marriage and is having an affair. Lisa is not questioning her commitment to Peter; she is skeptical of whether or not that commitment is reconcilable with her "choices" to love another man. The scene ends with Lisa's thought, *I need to tell you something*. This is unspoken, and I would argue, is so to represent the compulsory imperative of monogamy and a need to keep infidelity a secret or "in the closet" as it were.

The title of the film and this first scene establish the story as a narrative of triangulation between one woman and two men. However, from the start, we see a departure from Sedgwick's love triangle. First, it is Lisa's agency in choosing to have an affair and her skepticism of compulsory monogamy that introduces triangulation. At this point, the men's relationship to each other is nonexistent. Lisa, not the two men, has created a narrative bond between Peter and the other man. Second, when Lisa thinks but does not speak about her lover, it is her infidelity that must remain unspoken and will become the binding force between Peter and the other man. She wants to tell him. However, in a mononormative world, she can't.

Lisa is missing through most of the rest of the film. We don't know where she has gone, but, given the opening scene and the unfolding narrative, we are led to believe that she has left Peter for the other man. Consistent with Sedgwick's homosocial triangle, Lisa's absence temporarily reduces her to an object of exchange between Peter and the other man. Her love and desire for each man recedes temporarily to become a signifier of the homosocial bond between the men.

While in Lisa's study late one night, Peter hears her cell phone ring. The caller leaves a voicemail message, and Peter listens to it. It is a man's voice saying that he knows that he shouldn't call, but he needs to hear her voice. His suspicion deepening, Peter opens her computer to search for clues about who the man might be. After looking at several photos of himself, Lisa, and Abigail, he finds a folder entitled "Love." The folder is password protected, and though Peter tries different passwords, including his name, Abigail's name, and several other possibilities related to their marriage, he fails to open it.

In the next scene, Peter is in his office with Lisa's laptop computer obsessively trying to open the "Love" folder. Earlier in the film, Abigail had informed Peter that Lisa placed a note for him in a pair of red pumps that she left on her desk. The note simply says, "Lake Como." When Peter types "Lake Como" in the password dialogue box, the folder pops open. Hundreds of pictures appear on the screen. As he clicks through the photos, we see Lisa with the other man, Ralph, played by Antonio Banderas. In some of the photographs, they are nude, expressing a playful and sexual intimacy, and the pictures were obviously taken by each other. Peter cannot stop himself from looking at the images and will return over and over again to the folder to gaze at the photographic evidence of Lisa and Ralph's love affair. The photos become an important trope in the narrative. While they symbolize Lisa's infidelity, they also become a vehicle by which Peter inserts himself into Lisa and Ralph's relationship. He is obsessed with who the other man is and, while the photos reveal what the man looks like, Peter's obsession is more about finding out the nature of their relationship. Much of the rest of the film is Peter's search for, discovery of, and emergent relationship with Ralph. With Lisa out of the picture, the narrative is about the men's relationship to each other as Lisa's partners.

There is no doubt that, when he first discovers the pictures of Lisa and Ralph, Peter sees Ralph as a rival. As he tells the tech person at his software company that he needs to find the owner of an IP address, he says, "He calls himself Ralph. I want to meet him. I want to kill him." Sedgwick's competitive love triangle is established, as is Peter's embodiment of hegemonic masculinity. Using violence to eliminate the other man is one way to reclaim Lisa, regain his own masculine pride, and establish dominance over Ralph. That Lisa is gone from the narrative except in flashbacks suggests that she has no relevance. She is the relatively insignificant character that acts as the fulcrum between the two male rivals—the feminine object of exchange that binds the men together. However, as the narrative unfolds, Peter's relationship to Ralph becomes not about possessing Lisa, but instead, about learning who Lisa is by seeing her through the other man's eyes, and more important, seeing the other man through Lisa's eyes.

Peter's employee locates Ralph's IP address in Milan, a city where Lisa has often traveled as a shoe designer. Peter drops everything to go to Milan to find and kill Ralph. Rather than tracking him down and killing him, however, Peter follows Ralph into a café and challenges him to a game of chess. Though chess is a competitive duel to be sure, it is not a death challenge and, instead, offers ample time for conversation. Ralph is unaware that Peter is Lisa's husband, which provides Peter the opportunity to find out about Ralph and Lisa's relationship.

While the chess game pits the men as opponents, their conversation weaves in and out of exchanges of intimacy. For instance, Ralph describes the first time he met Lisa. He begins by saying, "It seems incredible. But all I saw was the shoes." We are then shown a flashback from Ralph's perspective. He gazes at her shoes, the red pumps in which Lisa placed the note reading "Lake Como," the password to the folder containing pictures of her and Ralph. His eyes move up her entire body to her face. Lisa says, "I make shoes. You?" Ralph smiles and replies, "I'm interested in poetry, and therefore, feet." Peter asks how long ago they met, and Ralph says that they met twelve years ago and last saw each other nine months ago, establishing that this is a long-term relationship that has lasted over a decade. Peter flashes back to Lisa returning from Milan. He asks her, "How was Milan?" She answers, "Lovely. Fun. I'm so happy to see you." Peter then recalls their conversation at dinner when she said, "It's a choice, not a promise. You meet someone. You fall in love. You have the opportunity. You make a choice."

In another conversation, Ralph and Peter are walking together. Peter asks Ralph, "Ever met a woman you'd like to live with?" Ralph responds, "Plenty of women desperate to live with me. But I don't live with anyone. See them often for lengthy periods, but not live." Ralph then asks Peter, "Married long?" Peter replies, "Nearly twenty-five years. We've both had separate careers, with all that that means. We've had a good marriage. Always trusted each other. Never doubted." Ralph smiles and says, "That's fine. Grand. But not for me. There's always doubt, my friend. Marriage is hell, as I'm sure you have found. I prefer hotels and heaven."

Peter is the husband and Ralph is the lover. By juxtaposing the "separate careers" in a long-term relationship and the distance it creates on the one hand with Ralph's interest in Lisa's shoes, poetry, hotels, and heaven on the other, Ralph and Peter come to embody different masculinities. Peter is the rational, calm, if somewhat cold husband, while Ralph is the romantic who loves art and poetry. This is not the only difference between Peter and Ralph. Peter runs a large software company, while Ralph is a building custodian. At first Ralph appears to be upper middle class—sporting an expensive tailored suit, playing chess, and talking about how he has traveled the world. It is more than halfway through the film when Peter discovers Ralph's actual occupation.

As Esther Saxey (2010) suggests in her analysis of compulsory monogamy in fiction, the two rivals in a WMM love triangle often embody different but valued masculine characteristics. Triangulation is resolved by the discovery that one man embodies all of the valued characteristics, allowing the woman to make the "right choice" to form a monogamous dyad. Peter is a wealthy British entrepreneur and Ralph is a working-class Spaniard. Peter—cold, rational, and possessive—embodies hegemonic masculinity, while Ralph is the sentimental, affectionate, and artistic lover.[1] Although the stark differences between them appear to be a reproduction of the trope Saxey describes, Lisa's absence forecloses the possibility that one man will be revealed to embody all of the desired characteristics and allow her to choose one over the other.

Though absent from the real-time relationship between Ralph and Peter, Lisa is present in the narrative through flashback. Immutable because it is what has already transpired and cannot be changed, Lisa's character comes alive and her choices begin to make sense. Through flashbacks, the audience is encouraged to identify with Lisa and to begin to understand why she wanted both men for her fulfillment of different needs.

Lisa also is present in a queer twist to the narrative when Peter, pretending to be her, begins replying to Ralph's emails. The slippage between Peter's and Lisa's subjectivities in the email exchanges is significant, opening narrative space for Peter to put himself in Lisa's shoes as Ralph's lover even as they remain adversaries. He begins to try to imagine what she sees in Ralph and what it was like for her to be Ralph's lover. At one point, Peter reads aloud to his daughter, Abigail, an email reply written by Ralph. He says, "What was she thinking? What sort of woman believes that sort of crap? How could she? . . . I wasn't enough for her. I'm so bloody angry I could kill him. I was always faithful to her. I thought we were close. I thought we told each other everything. But she was a different person. She must have been. Which is worse? The person you love is someone else with another man or they're the same. It's so bloody insulting."

The romance in Lisa's relationship with Ralph is unimaginable to Peter. He cannot wrap his mind around her ability to "believe" Ralph's love and sentimentality. Not only does this underscore the differences between the men—Peter is the predictable, pragmatic husband while Ralph is the romantic, passionate lover—it also means that Peter is putting himself in Lisa's place *in relationship to Ralph*. The rivalry and ho-moeroticism that are held in opposition in Sedgwick's homosociality collapse in to each other, and in that collapse, a queer closeness emerges as a feature of Ralph and Peter's relationship. Rather than sublimating homoerotic desire, triangulation between Peter, Ralph, and Lisa *creates* a queer identification and closeness between the men.

Meanwhile, Peter cannot stop looking at the intimate pictures of Ralph and Lisa, further inserting him in to their love affair. He goes back to them and, as he gazes at the pictures, he flashes back to scenes in his relationship with Lisa and conversations with Ralph about his re-lationship with her. Ralph's descriptions of his relationship with Lisa get more explicit and intimate. In one scene, Peter is again looking through the photos and recalls a story told by Ralph. As Ralph begins to talk, we see a flashback depicting his memory. Lisa and Ralph are in bed together having what appears to be a post-coital conversation. Ralph says to Lisa, "The passion I give you. I can't be without you anymore. You can't be without me. If you leave me I'll crash." Lisa is calm but says, "You frighten me." To this, Ralph says passionately, "I will. Don't let it come to that." Lisa asks, "What else can I do?" Ralph responds with a question. "Who are you happiest with?" Lisa replies, "Now? This mo-ment. You. Soon I'll be happy with another." Angrily, Ralph says, "Him," referring to Peter. Lisa says, "Of course, him."

Here we get the first glimpse of Ralph and Lisa's relationship from Ralph's perspective. Ralph, like Peter, wants her to himself. In her re-sponse, Lisa refuses to be the object of exchange between the two men she loves and does so by expressing her desire to be happy with both of them. Her insistence on polyamory rather than a dyadic resolution establishes her subjectivity as the glue that binds the men together and displaces the competition between them. She is not willing to sacrifice her own desire and happiness to resolve triangulation in one of her lov-ers' favor. It is significant that this flashback happens as Peter is looking at the intimate photos of Lisa and Ralph. This inserts Peter into their relationship, not as the sympathetic cuckold, but as embedded within

Lisa's relationship with Ralph. He is there in the bed with them, not just in terms of their conversation, but also by looking at the photos and exchanging emails with Ralph as Lisa.

Again, this provides almost a mirror image to Sedgwick's love triangle. Instead of having homoerotic love for each other and displacing it through a competitive struggle over the same love object, this queer, homosocial relationship between Ralph and Peter is established through Lisa's desire and love for both men. The men's erotic relationship to each other does not hinge on their desire for each other, but instead, on the subjective desire of the woman they both love. Rather than being displaced through homosociality, the men's erotic relationship to each other *emerges through the narrative* and hinges on Lisa's subjectivity and insistence on having them both.

The connection between the men is fully realized when Peter mocks Ralph for thinking he is communicating with Lisa when in fact, it is Peter who is pretending to be Lisa. Ralph tells Peter that Lisa is the most beautiful woman in the world. Ralph says, "I now know, she is the only woman I could ever love." Moving his chess piece, Ralph says with a satisfied grin, "Check." Peter looks at Ralph with a mixture of satisfaction, compassion, and anger and says, "She wronged you, has she?" Ralph nods, "She has." Peter asks, "You spoke to her?" Ralph nods. "She has acknowledged my call." Knowing that it is not Lisa, but himself who has "acknowledged" his call, Peter laughs at Ralph. Ralph laughs with him but we know that the joke is on Ralph and at this point, we are encouraged to feel compassion for both men. Ralph then says, "Do you ride? You know with horses as with women, and of course, you know that, to have good hands it is essential. Checkmate." Infuriated, Peter throws the chess pieces to the floor and, as he storms out says, "How dare you?" Confused, Ralph simply says, "It's only a game of fucking chess."

While this scene is clearly about rivalry—not just the chess game, but also the idea that Ralph has "good hands"—the rivalry once again collapses into homoerotic identification when Peter says to his daughter, "Have you seen his hands? Disgusting hands." Abigail responds, "Oh, I don't know? I've seen the pictures. I think he has nice hands." Peter's disgust reveals an initial identification with Lisa being erotically caressed by Ralph's hands. Peter is forced to queerly identify with Lisa by putting himself in this position. Peter's identification with Lisa forms an erotic connection, if uncomfortable and disgusting for Peter, between Peter and Ralph. Rather than being sublimated through erotic competition, homoerotic identification emerges and is established between the men precisely because of Lisa's sexual desire and partnership to both men.

As described in chapter 1 and as theorized by Sedgwick, the competitive love triangle must be resolved by the elimination of the other man, not just because of a desire to possess and control the feminine sexual object, but also to *straighten* out this queer identification with the woman and her desire for the other man. In a narrative of consensual polyamory, in contrast, there is no straightening out through sole possession. Each man in the Vee reconciles the female partner's ongoing desire for the other man, not by eliminating him, but instead by reconfiguring his masculinity to accommodate him.

The Other Man as Metamour

The conclusion of the film solidifies the polyamorous Vee instead of producing a winner-take-all monogamous dyad. Posing as Lisa, Peter sets up a meeting with Ralph at Lake Como. In this long scene, Ralph assumes he is meeting Lisa at a restaurant only to find that Peter is sitting at the table instead. Confused, Ralph sits as Peter reveals that Lisa is his wife and that she has died of breast cancer. While the audience is encouraged to feel compassion for both men in this scene, compassion for Ralph emerges more fully because the audience, like Ralph, is finding out for the first time that Lisa is dead. More important, however, Ralph's character is filled in, not just through his relationship with Peter, but also through his love for and intimate knowledge of Lisa. Empathy for Ralph allows us to begin to see what Lisa loved about him, and as we do, her subjectivity is more fully realized as well.

Stunned, Ralph asks Peter what happened. Through flashback, we see several scenes of Lisa in her deathbed as Peter recounts her final months. It is in these scenes that Lisa's subjective desire eclipses the rivalry between the men, for she not only wants to have both men as her partners, she also arranges their meeting.

In one of these flashbacks, the meaning of the note in the red pumps that read "Lake Como" emerges as a signifier of Lisa's desire to bring the two men together. In one flashback, Lisa is close to death and talking to Peter. She says, "You know. I've been very happy with you Peter." He asks, "Where? Where were you happiest?" Because she has difficulty talking, she has a pad of paper and pencil with which to communicate. Peter suggests she write it down and says, "I bet it will be the same [place I was happiest]." After a pause, he suggests, "Write down someplace we've never been that I could take you to." Lisa says, "You could take me anywhere." We then see Lisa write "Lake Como" on a small piece of paper and ask Abigail to place it in the shoes on her desk. "It's for your father." When Abigail questions whether or not he will find it, Lisa says, "He'll find it."

By placing the note for her husband in the shoes on her desk, Lisa brings her work life (the shoes), her home life (they are placed on a table in the home she shares with Peter), her relationship with Peter (where she would like to go with him), and her relationship with Ralph (Lake Como) together. That the note is both the password to the pictures of her and Ralph and their "special place," *and* the place she and Peter have never been but where he might take her symbolizes Lisa's desire to bring the men together.

Lisa's desire is realized at her memorial where both Ralph and Peter offer toasts to her. Ralph toasts first and focuses on her love of shoes. When Ralph finishes with his toast, Peter slowly stands. The other mourners, mostly Lisa's work colleagues, are wary of what he might say. The moment is pregnant with anxious anticipation. Everyone fears that Peter will claim ownership of Lisa by challenging Ralph to a final duel.

Peter refers to Ralph and says, "Look at him. There he is. Ralph. We have Ralph." As Ralph looks up warily, Abigail touches Peter's arm and sternly says, "Dad," as if she is pleading with him not to make a scene. Peter looks at Abigail and then again at Ralph. He continues, "Our host. God bless him. And now, my toast. To Lisa. My wife . . . ." Looking at Ralph, he says, "Your friend. My love. To Lisa. And to our daughter, Abigail." Reaching beyond Abigail, Peter takes the hand of her fiancé, George, and shakes it with sincerity and acceptance.

Both Ralph's and Peter's toasts place Lisa in the center of their relationship, not as an object of exchange to sublimate their homoerotic desire for each other as Sedgwick found in English literary texts, but as the woman they both love and who brought them together. Moreover, Peter's toast not only maintains the focus on Lisa, it acknowledges her relationship to Ralph as part of what is worthy of honor. The competitive triangle is resolved as a polyamorous Vee and the men become metamours. Peter's hegemonic masculinity—in the form of proprietary ownership and rivalry with Ralph—unravels and is reconstituted as acceptance of Lisa's love of Ralph and, as he shakes George's hand, Abigail's love of her fiancé. In fact, his acceptance of Lisa's relationship with Ralph can be read as the gateway to his acceptance of George. No longer the masculine subject in relationship to feminine objects of possession, Peter finally accepts not only Lisa's relationship to Ralph, but also his polyqueer kinship with Ralph.

In the final scene, Peter and Abigail are waiting together in a train station. Peter says, "All that stuff about shoes. Ralph." Peter chuckles with affection. "Ralph. Appalling, dreadful, but . . . ." Abigail looks at Peter and asks, "Well?" Peter responds, "He was also rather wonderful. And so was she. She really did know me, didn't she? Us. Him." In this statement, Peter establishes that Ralph is "wonderful" and, I would argue, a part of the family. By saying, "She really did know me. . . . Us. Him," Peter connects all three of them through *Lisa's* subjective knowledge of and desire for both men. In the end, they are all together.

After Peter says this, Abigail tentatively rests her head on his shoulder for a moment. He smiles and she leans on him. This is the first time we see any tenderness or affection between Peter and Abigail, further signifying a transformation of his masculinity.

They both stand and descend an escalator down to their train. The camera remains in the same location as Peter and Abigail recede. Suddenly George appears in the frame. He is holding three cups of coffee and, bewildered, looks around for Peter and Abigail. Seeing them below, he runs down the escalator. When he reaches them, Peter steps to the side and George moves in between Abigail and Peter. The film ends with the three of them walking off together. This final scene signifies that Peter's acceptance of Ralph is not just about Ralph but is also a transformation in Peter's masculinity. Peter's transformation through his acceptance of the other man has eliminated the jealousy he felt over George and allowed him to accept George *as Abigail's choice*. Peter is no longer the jealous, pragmatic, rational, calculating man he was in the beginning of the film. He finds Ralph "wonderful" and no longer feels the need to claim ownership or property rights to Lisa's love or his daughter's choice of partner. He is, in other words, no longer the embodiment of hegemonic masculinity.

In the end, Peter symbolically accepts Ralph as Lisa's other partner. By weaving Peter and Ralph's conversations with scenes of each of them with Lisa, the narrative transforms a love triangle into a polyamorous Vee. This is accomplished through the narrative insertion of Lisa's subjective desire to be lovers with both men as the bond between them. Because of Lisa's insistence on polyamory and his inability to change it, Peter must let go of the idea of having sole possession of her.

Moreover, the men develop an intimate, though not explicitly sexual, relationship with each other that hinges on Lisa's insistence on loving them both. This relationship subverts the subject/object and proprietor/property relationship between masculinity and femininity because neither man "owns" or controls Lisa's body or sexuality. Furthermore, the men have a shared erotic intimacy with each other through Lisa, not because they desire each other, but because they both desire and love her. Peter's recognition and acceptance of the "other man" is both represented by and accomplished through a queering of his relationship to Ralph *and to masculinity*. To the extent that heteromasculinity is defined by a man's possession and control of the feminine sexual object and competition with male rivals, this film queers masculinity through polyamory. Stated another way, polyamory or the acceptance of the "other man" disrupted the heteromasculine homosocial bond between Peter and Ralph and transformed it into something else. Significantly, the homosocial bond is queered not by bringing the two men's erotic desire for each other to the fore, but instead by situating Lisa as the desiring subject who refuses monogamy. The gendered structure of homosociality described by Sedgwick no longer holds up because of the introduction of polyamory into the narrative. The "other man," in other words, offers a glimpse into how narratives of *polyqueer homosociality* might open up an opportunity to signify a shift in gendered power relations.

The Love That Dares Not Speak Its Name

Until quite recently, gay and lesbian characters in film were never explicitly named as gay or lesbian or claimed a gay or lesbian identity, but for members of the audience in the know, it was obvious. Too often these "queer" characters were rendered as pathetic or evil and killed off symbolically or literally to straighten out the narrative, or they made their appearances as comedic relief to encourage the audience to identify with the heterosexual main characters. Queer audiences recognized them, and despite the negative stereotypes and maltreatment of these characters, often felt both hailed and disappointed.

As a polyamorous film enthusiast, I often feel hailed and disappointed when I watch films and television shows that are on the edges of or hint at polyamory, but in the end kill it off to establish the mononogamous couple. Watching *The Other Man* for the first time was different. Unlike most films that include erotic triangulation in the plot, *The Other*

Man, in a delicious and unexpected twist, kills off mononormativity so that polyamory can survive. And it does so by reconfiguring hegemonic masculinity into something a bit more polyqueer. At the same time, nowhere in this decidedly polyamorous film does any character say the word "polyamory" or name themselves or their relationship as polyamorous.

The film has a polyamorous resolution, but the word "polyamory" is as conspicuously absent as Lisa. It is, in the end, a polyqueer narrative of homosocial bonding that dallies around the edges of, if not straightforwardly represents, a polyamorous Vee, but in its silence about what the audience is witnessing, the film renders invisible polyamory as an intelligible relationship form. The disavowed polyamory is in plain sight, as it were. In other words, in the contemporary context of LGBT media visibility, it is not homoerotic desire that is the love that dares not speak its name. It is polyamory.

Conclusion

Writing about Noël Coward's 1932 play *Design for Living*, John Clum (1994) uses Sedgwick's theory of homosocial bonds to argue that its story is about two men who are homosexual and desire each other. However, because of the heterosexist necessity to sublimate homoerotic desire in British literature as described by Sedgwick, the characters in this early-twentieth-century play cannot *be* homosexual, but instead, bond through their shared relationship with the same woman. Homosexual desire, Clum argues, is straightened out by the presence of the woman and the homosexual men's platonic relationship with her.

Arguing that Clum's reading is "homosexist" because it ignores bisexuality and polyamory in the play, Sam See (2004) reads *Design for Living* as a narrative about a WMM triad in which everyone sleeps with everyone. See also reads the play as a portrayal of localized queer community making in not only a heterosexist, but also a biphobic and mononormative society. Agreeing with See and bringing Sedgwick back in, I read *Design for Living*, like *The Other Man*, as a narrative of *polyqueer homosocial bonding*, and as such, neither heterosexist or sexist, but instead, decidedly feminist and queer.[2]

I want to suggest that, in the mononormative context of contemporary film, polyamory and polyqueer desire (that is, a desire for polyqueer relationships rather than monogamy) are sublimated as not so much rivalry, but instead infidelity in need of a resolution. Infidelity narratives have emerged to replace or at least contest the narratives of competitive and sometimes deadly rivalry between men. Rather than render women objectified property and the predicate to men's homosocial bonds with each other, infidelity narratives allow women characters to be desiring subjects with agency. However, at the same time, mononormative narratives of infidelity need a monogamous resolution—one in which the woman does the choosing, but chooses one man over the other—a resolution that does not necessitate changes in or reconfigurations of masculinity and its representation.

In the end, *The Other Man* brings the sublimated desire for loving more than one person to the surface but does not call it polyamory. Perhaps this reflects nascent changes in our relationship to monogamy and an unspoken expectation if not tolerance of infidelity within the context of long-term monogamous relationships. However, rendering polyamory as the love that dares not speak its name also reflects the lack of queer and feminist critiques of mononormativity and the erasure of polyamory.

Finally, *The Other Man* also articulates and represents cultural shifts in gendered sexualities that emerged from late-twentieth- and early-twenty-first-century feminist theory and politics. Lisa has an affair made possible by her professional life, which includes long stretches of time away from home. In this contemporary feminist narrative, the woman is the desiring subject and, to the extent the men want to be intimately involved with her, each must reconfigure their masculinities in order to incorporate the "other man" into not just their relationships with Lisa, but also into their own understanding of themselves as men. Lisa's desire for both men is intelligible and, in the end, understandable and acceptable. Her agency in bringing them together and the explicit portrayal of the men's willingness to accept each other could not have been imaginable when Sedgwick wrote *Between Men*.

At the same time, Lisa, our strong, independent, desiring female character is, for most of the film, dead and appears only in flashback. She was not there with Peter and Abigail at the train station and never heard how Peter came to feel about Ralph and her relationship with him. Lisa was tragically absent when George joined Peter and Abigail to catch their train home.

But is Lisa's absence necessary?

Imagine if, instead of toasts to memorialize Lisa after her death, Lisa is alive and Peter and Ralph make their toasts at Abigail and George's wedding?[3] What if this scene does not create tension through the attendees' concern over Ralph and Peter's rivalry, as it did at Lisa's memorial, but instead does so with the wedding guests' confusion over the nature of the intimacy between Ralph and Peter as metamours? What if, in their toasts, the men honor Abigail and George, their bond with each other, wish them a long and happy life together, and remind them that marriage does not foreclose the possibility of intimacies with others? Monogamy, they might say, is a choice, not a foregone conclusion.

In the final scene, I can imagine Lisa there on the train platform with Peter and Abigail. She listens to Peter talk about how "wonderful" Ralph is. She sees the intimacy between Peter and Abigail as their daughter rests her head on his shoulder. Lisa's cell phone rings, and excusing herself, she says, "It's Ralph. Do you mind if I take the call?"

When she returns, she tells her family that Ralph sends his love and is looking forward to coming to visit soon and seeing them again.

As they descend the escalator and join George, Ralph is not immediately present, but he is there in all of their futures as they are in his, and the audience cannot *wait* for the sequel. Some members of the audience even imagine the hot man-on-man-on-woman action possible in a pornographic spoof of the film entitled something like "Doing the Other Man" (a topic I pick up in the next chapter).

What if, in other words, polyamory emerged from the shadows and was explicitly acknowledged and named as the plot resolution? What if, indeed.

4

The Heteromasculine Body and the
Threesome Imaginary

Exploring the Polyqueer Potential of Plural
Sexual Interactions

Paula had an unhappy and tumultuous family background;
in threesomes she seeks to control the men and the situation, and to create a bath of group love for herself. Despite
her sharp mind and powerful personality, and the fact that
her husband is younger, less experienced, and less asser-
tive than she, she hasn't been able to get men to do what
she wants—make love with each other as well as with her.
(240)
—Arno Karlen (1988)

What I want to pursue here . . . is the question of how erotic
practice stands to the negotiation of subjectivity within relations between men and women. If sex can be regarded
as a kind of theatre where subjective negotiations between
men and women are played out, then the choreography
of sexual encounters—what counts as active and passive,
whose boundaries are breached, who gives and who takes
pleasure—tells us something about these negotiations.
(267)
—Catherine Waldby (1996)

Can work on "desire" be antiracist work? Can antiracist
work *think* desire? (3)
—Sharon Holland (2012)

Introduction

As a jazz band plays in the corner of the dimly lit back patio of Bacchanal, my friend—a married, heterosexual white man in his forties—and I sip wine and catch up on each others' lives. He lives in a different city, and though we had spent much of our childhood together, we lost touch until we reconnected on Facebook, and he came to New Orleans for a convention.

After finishing half the bottle, he sheepishly smiles, leans in closer to me, and says, "Can I tell you something? I've wanted to tell someone about this for so long, and I have a feeling you'll enjoy this."

I take a sip of my wine, and with some trepidation, say, "Sure."

He looks around to see if anyone is within earshot, and then says, "I had a threesome with my wife and another woman."

While the fact that he had a threesome with his wife and another woman is surprising, for he seemed to be very conservative on Facebook, that he tells me is not.

I am "out" about being open, polyamorous, and into threesomes in my Facebook posts. He isn't the first straight-identified man to tell me that he desired or had a threesome with two women.

"Wow. Good for you. How was it?"

He leans back in his chair and sighs a huge, satisfied grin. "Awesome. Fantastic. I mean, it's every guy's dream, right? A threesome with two beautiful women."

"Well, maybe every straight guy's dream."

He looks puzzled for a moment, and then laughs. "Yeah, I guess you're right."

"So?" I play the good listener and open up an opportunity for him to talk about it.

"I was so surprised. It was my wife's idea and she pretty much set up the whole thing." Again he laughed. "There were times when I didn't really know what to do. You know? I was like a third wheel."

This time I laugh. It isn't the first time I heard this as well. "Sort of like moving to the rhythm of a jump rope and finding the right moment to jump in?"

"Exactly! They were obviously really into each other." He pauses and looks off and, I assume, was remembering how it all played out. "Don't get me wrong. I didn't mind. You know, just watching. But sometimes I felt sort of left out."

"That's not unusual, you know. Don't take it personally. Especially if Jan [his wife] set it all up. I'm guessing she's been into the idea of having sex with a woman for awhile?"

His brow creases with concern. "I guess so. Yeah. Now that I think about it, that's probably true. It was pretty hot, though."

"I'm sure! Like you said, 'every guy's dream.'" I let that last statement settle for a moment and then ask, "Would you ever have a threesome with your wife and another man?"

Without hesitation, he firmly says, "No way."

I smile. "Why not?"

"I'm not gay. No way. Besides, I couldn't handle seeing my wife have sex with someone else. No fucking way."

My friend winced at the idea of a threesome with another man because, as he put it, he couldn't stand to see his wife have sex with someone else. It is ironic that he could make this statement without any cognitive dissonance after telling me about achieving "every guy's dream" by having a threesome with his wife and another woman, especially when much of the time, apparently, his wife and the other woman were playing with each other rather than him. However ironic, it is neither unexpected nor contradictory that my friend rejected the idea of having a threesome with his wife and another man *and* proudly relished a threesome with another woman if we consider gender.

In a twenty-year study published in 1988, psychologist Arlen Karlen interviewed and had informal or clinical conversations with men and women who had participated in or rejected an invitation to a threesome. The majority of his research participants were involved in the swinger scene in the 1960s and 1970s, and although dated (more about this later), the research provides some insight into how gender structures threesomes.

In Karlen's sample, the majority of threesomes involve a man and two women (MWW). In most cases, the woman would initiate or suggest a MWW threesome because of her bisexual desire or curiosity, as was the case with my friend, or as a "gift" to the husband. Less often, the husband would initiate out of his own desire to fulfill a fantasy or to experience sexual pleasure with a new partner.

Regarding MWW threesomes, Karlen concludes that, despite a taboo against group sex, they can be a positive experience for those involved, because both women and men report satisfaction, pleasure, and a boost to self-esteem. Men in the sample described feeling a sense of control, power, and accomplishment in being able to satisfy two women at once and enjoying the excitement of having sex with someone new. For the women, threesomes with another woman, though sometimes fraught with jealousy or insecurity, often led to higher self-esteem as a result of pushing through fear and doing something taboo and risky. The women Karlen interviewed also reported experiencing more sexual pleasure, sometimes having their first orgasm, a stronger sense of entitlement to erotic desire, and a feeling of affection for—even, in some cases, an emotional bond with—the other woman.

Threesomes that involve a woman and two men (WMM), in contrast, are both rare and difficult according to Karlen. "Two to three times more men than women have homosexual experience, yet the majority of threesomes involve two women. When two-male triads do occur, the men usually take turns with the woman or pleasure her simultaneously, without homosexual contact. . . . If there is, as a few people claim, increasing male 'bisexuality' in threes and groups, the people I talked to haven't been part of it or seen it" (237). The two main reasons the men in Karlen's study gave for rejecting WMM threesomes were (1) a fear of or distaste for homoerotic contact with other men, and (2) performance anxiety and competition with another man. "Many men, and women as well, warned against threesomes involving two men, fearing that their competition would be unpleasant or explosive" (237–238).

When threesomes involving two men and a woman did occur, it was not because the men desired it, but because the woman did. In the quote by Karlen at the beginning of this chapter, he suggests that Paula, a woman who desired threesomes with two men, had an "unhappy and tumultuous family background," and therefore sought "to control the men and the situation" to fulfill her selfish desire to "create a bath of group love for herself" (240). Karlen concludes that, while some women might desire WMM threesomes, that desire is likely a result of an underlying and unresolved psychological conflict or problem. More important for my purposes here, Paula could not get the men to "make love with each other as well as with her" (240).

Karlen concludes that these gender differences result from biology and psychosexual development. Men do not desire threesomes with other males because of "the existence of a biological underpinning, stronger in males than females, for assertion, dominance, and rank-seeking. . . . [B]oth sexes tend to consider competitive success masculine, the penis and sexual penetration symbolic of power, being penetrated symbolic of passivity and subordination" (240). Once again, as we have seen in previous chapters, an evolutionary anthropological explanation is invoked to explain male sexual jealousy.

Karlen also looks to psychoanalytic theory when he concludes that men's rejection of WMM threesomes is inevitable because masculinity is dependent on its difference and distance from femininity. The presence of another man or a woman's insistence on involving another man in a sexual interaction will feel emasculating to a heterosexual man because of both the risk of homosexual contact and the possibility of being outperformed by another man. With the evolutionary anthropological and psychoanalytic explanations readily at hand, Karlen concludes that there is something natural and inevitable about men's distaste for threesomes with other men and women's ability to enthusiastically go with the flow in MWW threesomes.

As a sociologist, I am skeptical of Karlen's conclusions that differences in men and women's willingness to participate in threesomes are biological, let alone inevitable. First, the majority of Karlen's research participants were swingers, or in contemporary terms, in "The Lifestyle." Research on the swinging lifestyle consistently shows that the integrity of the couple is paramount. While swinger couples are non-monogamous in that they have sexual relations with other people, there are subcultural rules that prevent either member of such a couple from forming emotional attachments to others outside of the dyad. Possessiveness of one's partner, in other words, is still in play and it is more than likely that the gender structure of possessiveness described in chapter 1 would matter here as well, though perhaps in a diluted form.

Moreover, research on swinging subcultures shows that there are strong taboos against male bisexuality. Bisexual men in swinging subcultures report hostility from others, especially other men, but also from women about homoerotic contact among men (Frank 2008). In contrast, there is an assumption that most women are bisexual and bisexual women have higher social status than heterosexually identified women (Sheff 2005). Swingers' parties or clubs will often allow single women to attend but have strong restrictions on single men, ensuring that gender ratios work in the favor of MWW threesomes and not WMM encounters (Frank 2014). Heteronormative couple-centered swinging subcultures, in other words, feature structural and ideological constraints on expressing a desire for WMM threesomes.

It is likely that men and women who have a strong desire for WMM threesomes would find swinging communities and activities unsatisfying, if not hostile. To the extent that Karlen relied on snowball sampling and swingers' events, it is possible, if not likely, that his findings are an artifact of his sample and methods and not a valid and reliable picture of threesomes outside of swinging subcultures. This conclusion is even more probable when we consider another study of bisexuality in which the sample was drawn from a population in the San Francisco Bay Area and did not include swingers. Weinberg, Williams, and Pryor (1994) found that three men were the most common configuration for threesomes, followed by WMM threesomes. MWW threesomes were the least common gender structure. The contrast between Karlen's and Weinberg, Williams, and Pryor's findings suggests that social context matters. The meanings and experience of threesomes, like other areas of sexuality, are embedded within and constitutive of broader social structures, localized norms, and contextually specific interpersonal relations.

Sociological theory and research on sexuality has, for decades, shown that sex and sexuality, including the embodied desire for and experience of sex results from not just biological or psychological processes, but also, and importantly, social processes. If we consider threesomes from a sociological perspective—as resulting from and constitutive of social rather than or in addition to biological or psychological processes—perhaps Karlen's findings and my friend's disavowal of WMM threesomes have more to do with the social organization of gender, threesomes as gendered interaction, and the *threesome imaginary* as a reflection and articulation of gendered power relations than evolution or early childhood psychosexual development. By *threesome imaginary*, I mean collective fantasies or ideations about threesomes that define them in ways that reflect and maintain existing power relations and legitimize social privilege.

The Sexual Field, Erotic Habitus, and Power

In his essay on the sexual field and erotic habitus, Adam Isaiah Green (2008a) builds a sociological theory of desire that bridges the theoretical gap between sociological script theory and psychodynamic processes of sexual ideation or fantasy. His theoretical project is to explain how the external social structure of sexuality—circulating meanings and norms about the erotic and sexual relations—comes to be embodied by individuals as erotic desire.

Green suggests that Pierre Bourdieu's concepts *social field* and *habitus* are useful in this regard. According to Bourdieu, society is made up of a social field of multiple and interconnected social locations, collective meanings, and norms for behavior. One's class location in the social field will affect not just access to resources, but also access to particular experiences and interactions. As habituated conduct, those experiences will shape an individual's preferences, tastes, proclivities, and competencies so that class location becomes a somatic experience felt as "natural" despite being structured by the social field.

While Bourdieu focuses on class habitus, Green applies the concept to erotic desire. According to Green, the social structure includes circulating narratives and imagery of who is sexy and why, what he calls "erotic typologies" that are structured by race, class, and gender. Depending on one's location in the sexual field, different kinds of erotic ideations are available as fodder for sexual fantasies.

Over time and through habituated ideation, the socially constructed and circulating images and narratives come to feel "natural" as erotic desire emanating from within. This is, according to Green, erotic habitus.

> [Erotic habitus is] a socially constituted complex of dispositions, appreciations, and inclinations arising from objective historical conditions wherein, via symbolic force, the schemata of erotic passions are configured. Beneath the level of consciousness, the schemata of the erotic habitus—eroticized typologies revolving around classifications of race, class, and sex for instance—represent the "embedding of social structure in bodies" (Bourdieu 1998:40), lending sexual fantasy its collective and historical character. Hence, erotic habitus is a concept that relates the schemas of erotic fantasy to the social organization of society. (30)

One's location in the social structure, including but not limited to race, class, sexual identity, and gender, will affect the sorts of erotic meanings to which individuals are exposed and attend, and as such, will play a role in shaping their erotic schemata in the form of fantasy. Erotic habitus then, like class habitus, will be shared or have a similar structure for individuals who occupy similar locations in the sexual field.

One of the most significant structuring and stratifying features of the sexual field is gender. A network of meanings about gender difference and social hierarchies structure the sexual field so that men and women have access to different erotic fantasies and ideation and are situated by others differently in terms of fantasy and erotic ideation. Through repeated exposure to those gendered meanings, men and women incorporate them into their sense of gendered self as embodied erotic "inclinations, dispositions, schemes of actions and appreciations" (Green 2008b, 599).

Hegemonic masculinity and femininity and the structure of power relations between them, then, are not just a set of external social rules or scripts that individuals consciously accept or reject; they are incorporated into the body as subconscious desires and fantasies. Heterosexual men, for instance, will have in common certain erotic fantasies about women and women's bodies, and to the extent that those fantasies resonate with the social construction of women's bodies as sexy in particular ways, the fantasies are deeply social and constitutive of the heteromasculine erotic habitus. Likewise for heterosexual women and the hetero-feminine erotic habitus.

Importantly, Green points out that erotic desire is not determined or eclipsed by the external social structure. There are aspects of desire that do not originate in the realm of the social, but perhaps in other non-sociological factors such as the idiosyncratic biography of individuals' psychology or biology. However, despite the aspects of desire that are beyond the social, what is incorporated from the social and sexual field is deeply sociological and falls under the purview of sociological theory and analysis rather than psychology or psychoanalysis.

While Green focuses on the kinds of people we fantasize about and/or desire, erotic schemata would include not just body typologies, but also kinds of sexual practices, experiences, and interactions. According to Schilt and Windsor (2014), it is not only fantasies that are structured by location in the sexual field, but also access to sexual or erotic experiences and interactions. In their research on transgender embodiment, Schilt and Windsor found that transgender individuals' embodied desire and access to sexual experiences, what they call the *sexual habitus*, shifted over time as they transitioned from one gender status to another. As their gender location in the sexual field changed, the transgender men they interviewed reported experiencing fantasies about and having access to sexual experiences they did not prior to transitioning. Schilt and Windsor argue that sexual habitus is linked to, but separate from, erotic habitus. One can fantasize about a particular sexual experience, but whether or not there are partners available to fulfill that fantasy will be structured by one's location in the sexual field and how it situates an individual in relationship to others.

From a sociological perspective, then, my friend's strong reaction to the idea of a threesome with his wife and another man, though felt in the body as repulsion, is in part structured by his location in the sexual field as a heterosexual man. The question here is, what, if anything, is *social or sociological* about threesomes as erotic fantasy and social interaction, and what role do heteromasculinityand mononormativity play in the meaning of and access to threesomes as part of the sexual field?

Mononormativity and the Threesome Imaginary

A largely undertheorized and central structuring feature of the sexual field is mononormativity and its insistence on, not just couple relationships, but also one-on-one sexual interactions. The sexual field includes a network of symbolic meanings and assumptions about "good sex", both in terms of morality and pleasure that is deeply mononormative in that sex between two partners is the ideal standard. As described by Rubin (1975), the charmed circle of sexual normalcy defines one-on-one sex between committed partners as "good," as in moral, while sexual interactions that include more than two people are considered deviant,

relegated to the perverse, and cast outside the charmed circle of normative sexual interactions.[1]

At the same time, because group sex is considered taboo and "perverse," it is also highly eroticized and readily available as fantasy. As such
and as part of the *mononormative* sexual field, fantasies about sexual
threesomes are embedded within and reiterative of the social structure,
including compulsory monogamy. For instance, threesomes are considered a relatively acceptable way for a couple to take a walk on the wild
side when the encounter is framed as a momentary suspension of normalcy. They are far less acceptable if constitutive of a sexual orientation
(e.g., *my sexual preference is for threesomes rather than dyadic sex*) or as a
recurring or structuring aspect of intimate relationships over time (e.g.,
we are a polyamorous triad and we all sleep in the same bed every night).
The occasional fantasy or once-in-a-lifetime experience of a threesome
with one's partner and a third party provides a temporary reprieve from
the monotony of long-term monogamy, and as such, releases some of the
pressure of monogamy without threatening the monogamous couple.

The fantasy of a temporary and occasional threesome, in other words,
serves mononormativity by opening ideational space to fantasize about
new partners while, at the same time, reifying the monogamous couple
as sacred. As Frank and DeLamater (2010) found, "monogamish" couples often fantasize together about threesomes with particular or imagined others as a way to "spice up" their sex life without violating the
norms of compulsory monogamy.

In this way, the fantasies of a threesome with real or imagined others
is, for some, part of the erotic habitus of couples. Situated in the mononormative sexual field, the threesome imaginary that constructs "acceptable" threesomes as a couple temporarily inviting an outside person into
their fantasies or less frequently, into their beds, reflects and maintains
the monogamous couple as the only acceptable and legitimate way to
do sexually and emotionally intimate relationships *and* threesomes. In
other words, both the threesome imaginary and the occasional three-

some are consistent with monogamy. The monogamous couple is so-
lidified and legitimated as the essential and normative unit by situating
threesomes as a temporary step outside rather than a legitimate orientation for individuals or structure for relationships. As philosopher of
the erotic Marco Vassi (2005) writes, "With two accepted as the ideal,
the 'natural' way of doing things, the other numbers get relegated to the
categories of sin, crime, perversion, or diversion" (287).

Gender and the Threesome Imaginary

While the threesome imaginary is available as a relatively harmless and
naughty bit of fun for couples, and thus reflective of the sexual field for
heterosexual women and men, there is a decidedly gendered structure to
the threesome imaginary. For couples, MWW threesomes are harmless,
hot fun, but a couple inviting another man into their sexual lives, even if
temporarily, is, if not unthinkable, imagined as thoroughly undesirable
by most heterosexual men. In other words, the heteromasculine erotic
habitus includes a strong disavowal of WMM threesomes with their
partners. The disavowal of a threesome with another man, though felt
as personal and embodied, is not just an expression of an internal and
essential sexual orientation, though asocial factors might also be at play.
Green's (and my) point is that, even if there is something psychological or even biological about this disavowal, it does not mean that social
structure does not play an important, even central role.

We might, for instance, point to music videos, films, and television
programs that use the trope of a threesome with two women to signify
a man's status. Show any man in bed with two or more women and not
only is he rendered powerful and high status, he supposedly becomes
the object of every straight man's envy. MWW threesomes are a staple in
pornography marketed to heterosexual men, and "lesbian" porn meant
to appeal to straight men consistently situates the viewer (assumed to
be a heterosexual man) as the desiring subject in relationship to the two
women.

A heterosexual man who fantasizes about and seeks a threesome with two women is as normal as normal can be. In fact, if a heterosexual man does not express desire for a MWW threesome, his sexual orientation and/or masculinity become suspect. In other words, a MWW threesome in which the man is the desiring subject and the women are objects of desire is a central feature of the sexual field and, as such, a readily available fantasy that can be incorporated into the heteromasculine erotic habitus.

Because heterosexual women are also exposed to the same images, messages, and meanings, MWW threesomes are also a part of the heterofeminine erotic habitus. The threesome imaginary assumes that a woman who desires or engages in a threesome with a man and another woman is not a closeted lesbian. For men like my friend, his wife's desire for a threesome with a woman might indicate bisexual desire or curiosity, but temporarily so and only sexually, not in terms of emotional intimacy or relationship commitment.

On the other hand, the sexual field does not include readily available discourses and imagery that eroticize WMM threesomes, sometimes referred to in colloquial terms as a "devil's threesome."[2] In fact, straight men are situated in the sexual field in ways that close off flows of desire toward threesomes with other men unless it is construed as a decidedly straight and objectifying "take-turns-on-the-girl" scenario or "hot-wifing,"[3] in which a husband watches his wife have sex with another man. In both scenarios, the men do not have sex with each other, and the woman is an erotic object of exchange between men. As Lewis (2010) found in her research on the cuckolding lifestyle, men are far more likely to introduce the idea of hot-wifing to their partners and most of them experience hot-wifing as proof of their manhood because, in the end, the woman belongs to the husband.

In her book on group sex, Katherine Frank (2013) discusses professional athletes' willingness to "share" women as way to bond with each other and level hierarchies that might compromise team solidarity. "Athletes who share women often display a surprising lack of jealousy toward teammates during these encounters—at least when it comes to women who fall into the 'share' category" (237). Women who are in the "share" category are generally groupies and not emotionally intimate partners with the athletes. In these sexual interactions and in "straight" porn, the woman is treated as an object of exchange through which the men bond with each other. Ensuring that there is little to no contact between the men is necessary in order to "straighten" out what could potentially be a very polyqueer encounter. In contrast, when men have sex with each other in porn featuring WMM threesomes, it becomes a completely different genre and is given the label "bisexual porn."[4]

In their recent study of threesomes, Scoats, Joseph, and Anderson (forthcoming) found that there is some evidence that the taboo against WMM threesomes is loosening. In their small sample of thirty straight-identified men, five had had a WMM threesome, and some of the men who had not expressed interest in or amenability to such an encounter. At the same time, the majority of those who said they would be interested in a WMM threesome said that they would do it only with their best friend, for reasons that revolved around trust, comfort with being naked, and homosocial bonding. While Scoats, Joseph, and Anderson suggest that this comfort with the idea—or actuality—of a WMM threesome involving a close friend reveals a cultural shift away from the "one-time rule of homosexuality" for straight-identified men (Anderson 2014), their study also shows that WMM threesomes are not a central feature of the heteromasculine erotic habitus.

In her book *Queer Phenomenology*, Sara Ahmed (2007) suggests that a heterosexual orientation is less about being attracted to certain kinds of people and more about being steered away from or clear of "queer objects."

Heterosexuality is [not] . . . then simply an orientation toward others, it is also something that we are orientated around, even if it disappears from view. It is not that the heterosexual subject has to turn away from queer objects in accepting heterosexuality . . . compulsory heterosexuality makes such a turning unnecessary (although becoming straight *can be* lived as a "turning away"). Queer objects, which do not allow the subject to approximate the form of the heterosexual couple, may not even get near enough to "come into view" as possible objects to be directed toward. . . . The body acts upon what is nearby or at hand, and then gets shaped by its directions toward such objects, which keeps other objects beyond the bodily horizon of the straight subject. (90–91; italics in original)

Sexual orientation is not a fixed place (identity); it is a position in relationship to and tending toward other objects. An orientation toward specific objects renders other objects invisible, out of reach, or insignificant.

Combining the sociological concepts of sexual field and sexual habitus with Ahmed's definition of sexual orientation, we might say that sexual orientation toward objects is not random or casual, but is organized by the sexual field that places some objects within reach and establishes lines of action that compel one toward certain objects and not others. If we expand the notion of "objects" from kinds of people to kinds of behaviors or sexual interactions, we might say that MWW threesomes are on a heteronormative line or orientation and WMM threesomes are situated as out of reach and off the "straight" line between heteromasculinity and heterofemininity. Mononormativity or the institutionalization of dyadic sex as the only normative way to erotically engage with others, combined with the social construction of MWW threesomes as a temporary and relatively harmless reprieve from monogamy, places WMM threesomes beyond the bodily horizon of heterosexual men and women within the sexual field.

This necessitates not just desire oriented toward MWW threesomes, but also a turning away from the possibility of a WMM threesome. For instance, pornography marketed to heterosexual men does not include WMM threesomes where men "get it on" with each other, as women routinely do in MWW porn. There are not readily available images of men gaining or demonstrating status by having a WMM threesome, and a straight man's expression of desire for a WMM threesome is likely to be met with ridicule and a loss of status.[5] To the extent that they are not a readily available narrative or fantasy in the heteromasculine or heterofeminine erotic habitus, WMM threesomes, unlike MWW threesomes, can be considered queer "objects" or sexual interactions. In Ahmed's terms, a heterosexual man's desire to invite another man into a heterosexual interaction with himself and his partner constitutes a queer erotic orientation away from the mono- and heteronormative threesome imaginary.

I want to suggest that a desire for WMM threesomes constitutes a queer erotic orientation for heterosexual women as well. Although the temporarily "bisexual" experience of a MWW threesome is normatively acceptable for heterosexual women, having desire for or an experience of group sex with two or more men is not. While a man who has a threesome with two women is considered "lucky" and high in status, a woman who has sex with more than one man is often perceived as victimized or a slut. Katherine Frank (2013) writes, "Women's participation in group sex, especially encounters involving many men, is often skeptically or simplistically attributed to coercion or psychological dysfunction" (239).

What is it about masculinity and femininity that is being played out in the dominant threesome imaginary? Referring back to the observation of Catherine Waldby's (1996) quoted at the beginning of this chapter, I'm interested in unpacking how threesomes, as a "theatre where subjective negotiations between men and women are played out . . . tell[] us something about these negotiations" (267). Whose interests are reflected and served in the dominant threesome imaginary? What might the gender structure of the threesome imaginary tell us about the subjective negotiations between men and women?

The Impenetrable Heteromasculine Body

In a provocative essay linking heteromasculine power with impenetrability, Waldby suggests that the sexual field situates men and women differently in relationship to what she calls "erotic destruction." Adopting a feminist and psychoanalytic framework to develop a theory of the gender structure of erotic destruction, Waldby describes it as

> a . . . momentary annihilation or suspension of what normally counts as "identity," the conscious, masterful, self-identical self, lost in the "little death" of orgasm. These momentary suspensions, when linked together in the context of a particular relationship, work towards a more profound kind of ego destruction . . . each lover is refigured by the other, made to bear the mark of the other upon the self. But all such transformation involves the breaking down of resistance, of violence to an existing order of the ego. (266–267)

For Waldby, the erotic offers an opportunity for destruction, both in terms of the temporary loss of boundaries between self and other during the ecstasy of orgasm and in terms of incorporating another into the structure of the self over time in an intimate relationship. To experience erotic destruction does not mean being completely destroyed in any kind of negative sense. Instead, it involves ecstatic pleasure through orgasm and the forming of bonds through intersubjective intimacy, and it is something most humans desire and seek.[6]

However, because of the social organization of gender, sexuality, and violence, there is a gender structure to *the meaning of* bodily penetration and destruction within the context of heterosexuality. Men are assumed to destroy women; women can never destroy men. Heteromasculinity is constituted by an impenetrable sovereign subjectivity and the male body is assumed to be essentially different from the female body in that it is inviolable. Heterofeminine subjectivity and embodiment, in contrast, is constructed as permeable and thus fluid. According to Waldby,

> The culture's privileging of masculinity means that the hegemonic bodily imago of masculinity conforms with his status as sovereign ego, the destroyer, and that of women with the correlative status of the one who is made to conform to this ego, the destroyed. The male body is understood as phallic and impenetrable, as a war-body simultaneously armed and armoured, equipped for victory. The female body is its opposite, permeable and receptive, able to absorb all this violence. In other words, boundary difference is displaced outwards from (imaginary) genital difference. . . . In this way the genital markers of sexual difference, the penis and the vagina, seem to render the kinds of power relations attendant upon them as natural and inevitable. (268)

Men must remain sovereign, immutable selves during sexual intercourse and in relationships, while women are expected to physically and psychically acquiesce to men's subjectivity and bodies and, in order to do so, surrender or remake the self so as to accommodate penetration into their bodies and identities.

The hegemonic and constructed relationship between masculinity and femininity, then, includes a set of eroticized binaries that situate the masculine as superior and dominant along the lines of destroyer/destroyed, impenetrable/penetrable, and active insertion/passive receptivity. As a mimetic manifestation of a male-dominant social structure in which men are sovereign subjects, erotic destruction takes on a gender structure in which men destroy women and women are destroyed. Heteromasculinity is constructed and experienced as more than just active in relationship to feminine passivity; it is also embodied as impenetrability in relationship to feminine penetrability. Here Waldby dovetails with Green when she argues that these constructions are not simply external meanings floating outside of bodies, but instead come to be a somatic experience for women and men.

While Arno Karlen and evolutionary anthropologists suggest that men are naturally dominant because they penetrate, Waldby disagrees. The *meaning* of penetration as a relation of domination is a gendered social construction to legitimate and naturalize men's social power. The social construction of men's bodies as impenetrable and female bodies as violable is, in other words, established and perpetuated through circulating meanings and normative heterosexual scripts and practices in the sexual field.

Because heterosexual men and heterosexual women are situated differently within the sexual field, they will tend to have differing fantasies and desires around relations of insertion and receptivity, but that difference is social, not anatomical or biological. As Waldby reminds us, there is nothing inherently impenetrable about the male body. Anal penetration is not only possible; it can be and often is deeply pleasurable for male-bodied individuals.

Despite the potential for embodied and erotic pleasure through anal penetration, there are strong, stigmatizing taboos against anal receptivity for heteromasculine subjectivity and embodiment. This link between body, identity, and desire and the taboo against anal penetrability is so pervasive that heterosexual men often believe that if they experience pleasure through anal stimulation it means that they might be gay . Because the sexual field saturates homosexual identity with anal receptivity, any sort of anal play or penetration, even with a woman, is often interpreted as an indication of an underlying homosexual desire and identity (Branfman and Stiritz 2012; Guss 2010; Melby 2005). This aspect of the sexual field would explain the existence of a sort of "one drop rule" concerning homoerotic desire or sex with another man. Any homoerotic experience indicates an essential gay self, and to the extent that homosexuality is feminizing, heteromasculine subjectivity depends on a thorough rejection of anal receptivity.

Consistent with Green's notion of erotic habitus, Waldby argues that heterosexual men's embodied revulsion at the idea of anal penetration is both real and has a social origin. Instead of being grounded in biology or anatomy, it is a manifestation of gendered power relations. The impenetrable heteromasculine body is constructed as inherently different from women's and gay men's bodies in order to punctuate an illusory binary and legitimate social hierarchies that situate heteromasculinity as dominant and superior to heterofemininity and homosexuality. The heteromasculine erotic habitus, then, consists of a rather violent rejection of the idea of anal penetration. Anal penetration is "out of reach" or out of line with heteromasculinity and thus restricted solely to women's and gay men's bodies.

This offers a sociological explanation for the exclusion of WMM threesomes in the threesome imaginary. Another man in the bed introduces the possibility of being taken as the object of desire by another man, *feeling* excitement or desire in relationship to another man, and the specter of being anally penetrated—all of which threaten not just heteromasculine subjectivity, but also heteromasculine power. This would explain why, when I asked my friend if he would have a WMM threesome with his wife, he said, "I'm not gay."

Moreover, when my friend said that he would not want to watch his wife have "sex with someone else" but enjoyed having a threesome with another woman, he revealed an underlying gendered understanding of sex as limited to penetration of another body by a penis. A threesome with two women means that only he would be in possession of a penis and thus situated comfortably as the penetrator, the doer, the destroyer, the impenetrable sovereign subject. Two women are not "empowered" to destroy him, but a man would be.

In addition, rendering a heterosexual woman's desire for WMM threesomes as pathological or as victimization closes off flows of desire toward WMM threesomes for women as well and resonates with the framing of heterofeminine sexual subjectivity as passive and violable. In this way, the sexual field situates MWW threesomes as deeply heterosexual and WMM threesomes as "gay" and solidifies heteromasculine subjectivity as dominant in relationship to women and gay men. As Marjorie Garber (2000) writes about threesomes, "Two men and a woman together . . . are clearly 'bisexual.' But they are also more culturally threatening than two women and a man, a triad that connotes 'mastery' and manliness (to men), but also voluptuous excess" (477).

Again, I want to reiterate that there is no anatomical or biological inevitability or imperative to the gender structure of penetration or to a WMM threesome being coerced or constituting victimization. As stated earlier, male bodies are penetrable and penetration can be physically pleasurable. The threesome imaginary closes off erotic ideation and flows of desire toward WMM not because of biological or anatomical inevitability, but instead to "protect" heterosexual men from the risk of erotic destruction and to ensure the illusion of the impenetrable heteromasculine body as different from and superior to the feminine or homosexual body.

Perhaps, on the other hand, my friend was afraid of being outperformed, and that is why he would never want to have a threesome with another man. Certainly, the threesome imaginary as reflected in Karlen's conclusions and evolutionary psychology would have us believe that there is something natural about a man's inability to conceive of "sharing" his wife with another man in a WMM threesome. As the destroyer, heterosexual men place a great deal of their sense of self-worth in their ability to "destroy" the heterofeminine body. Remember that "destruction" is the ecstatic loss of the boundary between self and other through orgasm. As Waldby (1996) suggests, for the heteromasculine body, this is felt as a need to "get the job done" with skill and precision. In this heteronormative construction, the man is the "doer" while the woman gets "done." Manipulate her body in the right way, and you'll "get her done."

While heteromasculinity includes possession, destruction, and getting the job done, heterofemininity is constructed as its complement—possessed, destroyed, and the job that gets done. However, the threat of another man getting the job done *as threat* reveals that "getting the job done" is less about women's pleasure and more about embodying heteromasculine mastery and control. After all, wouldn't another man in the bed *alleviate* pressure on an individual man to "get the job done"? The idea that another man is a rival rather than a cooperative partner is deeply objectifying, reinforcing the notion that the woman is a "job" to get done and vehicle for enhancing heteromasculine sexual subjectivity rather than a sexual subject with her own desires and agency and deserving of sexual pleasure in her own right.

Finally, to the extent that another man in the bed is understood as a competitor who might be more skillful and have better equipment to get the job done, the hegemonic threesome imaginary protects heterosexual men from any overt comparisons with other men. Dyadic heterosexual interactions, though often fraught with anxiety about performance for heterosexual men, do not raise the specter of actual competition and outperformance. Significantly and revealingly, the threesome imaginary that casts MWW threesomes as relatively harmless fun does not protect heterosexual women from this experience. Again, this reveals ways in which the threesome imaginary serves heteromasculine interests. Further, the narrative that men could never handle it but women could reinforces assumed gender differences between women and men that conflate masculinity with competition and aggression and femininity with cooperation and passivity. In sum, the hegemonic threesome imaginary as a structuring feature of the erotic and sexual field for heterosexual women and men does a great deal of ideological *and ideational* work to secure heteromasculine subjectivity, dominance, and privilege through the erotic habitus of straight men and women.

However, this is not inevitable. Green (2008b) writes, "[E]ven as the erotic habitus materializes early in psychological life, it is not to be conceived as an ossified psychic structure but, rather, subject to change over time as individuals have new experiences that reconstitute self-concept and the self's location in social space" (615). Social experience is equally if not more important than psychological therapy when it comes to reconfiguring the gender structure of the erotic habitus. Schilt and Windsor's (2014) research, discussed above, is further evidence that the erotic habitus can shift over time with exposure to new fantasies and sexual interactions.

Changes in gendered embodiment can also bring changes in sexual practices, identities, and partners. Trans men's gender, embodiment, erotic

ideation, and established repertoire of sexual practices and domain of potential partners—what we term "sexual habitus"—can be affirmed, transformed, or challenged as their personal sense of maleness or masculinity
becomes visible to others. Such transformations can be experienced as
exciting or as unsettling, as trans men grapple with learning new expectations and practices for their transformed sexual identity. Changes in
sexual habitus can lead trans men to rethink their desired gendered embodiment. This feedback loop between embodiment, practices, and identities illustrates how "gendered sexualities" . . . relate to physical bodies,
as well as how one's sexual habitus transforms across the life course. (745)

While there are important differences between the experiences of transgender individuals transitioning and heteromasculine embodiment,
Schilt and Windsor's research shows that erotic habitus is not fixed and
that exposure to new erotic experiences can have an effect on sexual
subjectivity.

Toward a Polyqueer Threesome Imaginary

Catherine Waldby (1996) argues that heteromasculine embodiment
can be reconfigured, at least partially, through the pornographic and/
or narrative eroticization of heteromasculine anal receptivity. Waldby
suggests that new narratives of a penetrable masculinity can shift not
just the embodied desire of individuals, *but also the gender structure of
the sexual field* so that a heteromasculine penetrable body can become
an available fantasy to be incorporated into both the heteromasculine
and heterofeminine erotic habitus. Writing about bisexuality, Marjorie
Garber (2000) states, "The question of whether someone was 'really'
straight or 'really' gay misrecognizes the nature of sexuality, which is
fluid, not fixed, a narrative that changes over time rather than a fixed
identity, however complex. The erotic discovery of bisexuality is the fact
that it reveals sexuality to be a process of growth, transformation, and
surprise, not a stable and knowable state of being" (66).

Recent sociological research on transgender embodiment like that of Schilt and Windsor shows that remaking the body in terms not just of gender display, but also the erotic is a central part of transitioning. As C. Jacob Hale (2002) discusses in his essay about SM practices in queer lesbian and transgender play spaces, sexual practices can remap the body. Hale writes, "leatherdyke genderplay enables a phenomenon sometimes called 'retooling' or 'recoding' our bodies in trans community discourse. Sexual interactions . . . are some of the sites at which dominant cultural connections between genitals and gender are the tightest, so many transpeople must remap the sexualized zones of our bodies if we are to be sexually active. Through leatherdyke SM practice, I was able to disrupt the dominant cultural meanings of my genitals and to reconfigure those meanings" (427).

Erotic embodiment, or the subjective experience of bodily sensations, is shaped by but also shapes gendered subjectivity. New experiences, like anal eroticism for heterosexual cisgender men, can "retool" or "recode" the heteromasculine body in ways that reconfigure heteromasculine subjectivity. Branfman and Stiritz (2012) agree when they suggest that sex education should include what they call "prostage" education—instruction on the pleasure male bodies can experience through prostate massage (prostage). They suggest, "prostage education can help challenge traditional norms of gender and sexuality [that] continue to misrepresent men's sexuality and colonize men's bodies. These norms constrain behavior and thought, even as some men come to espouse less rigid models of manhood. Prostage education can provide all people, not only men, tools and motivation to question the beliefs that underpin sexism, homophobia, and male dominance" (423–424).

Marco Vassi (2006) makes precisely this argument when he theorizes the relationship between subjectivity and non-dyadic sex. Threesomes, he suggests, are especially interesting in terms of gendered subjectivity. "Three must be understood as more than the addition of one more to the basic of two. It involves a whole new quality of consciousness, something which cannot come about with people who are still thinking in male-female terms" (Vassi 2005). Marco Vassi (2006) uses auto-ethnographic erotic narrative to illustrate how WMM threesomes confound gender and sexual identity.

> I was fucked while fucking. She lay under me in classic pose, her legs at a thirty-degree angle, her knees slightly raised as I swam in the hot moistness of her cunt easily. Suddenly he was on top of me with a stuttering shudder his cock soared between my buttocks and penetrated my flesh. As he moved into the privacy of my inner space of sensation, the basic question of all bisexuality came to the surface: how to be a man to the woman while being a woman to the man, and how to be a man to the woman while being a man to the man, and how to be a woman to the woman while being a woman to the man, and how to be a woman to the woman while being a man to the man? . . . I could not deal with the multiplicity of levels except by surrender. (12)

He concludes about experiencing a WMM threesome, "I lost my sexual identity and became a sexual entity" (12). We might say that what Vassi describes is the erotic destruction of heteromasculine embodiment and subjectivity.

While Vassi depicts a very polyqueer experience of a WMM threesome, individual men's experiences will do little to alter the gendered and racialized sexual field. As discussed above, Scoats, Joseph, and Anderson's (forthcoming) research suggests that straight-identified men are open to and have WMM threesomes, but only so long as there is minimal sexual contact between men. For these reasons, I am arguing that polyqueer cultural production where narratives, imagery, and subcultures in which polyqueer WMM threesomes are eroticized constitute a queer, feminist intervention in straight sexual culture.

The popularity of slash fiction among straight-identified women suggests that participation, at least as spectators, in erotic exchanges between men is already circulating in the sexual field and part of a heterofeminine erotic habitus. Slash fiction is a genre of erotic storytelling in which popular fictional narratives are rewritten so that ostensibly straight male characters fall in love with each other and express that love through homoerotic sex. Slash fiction began with straight women rewriting the relationship between *Star Trek* characters Kirk and Spock (Penley 1995). It is now a huge online subculture, and though there is increasing participation by gay and bisexual men, slash fiction is still dominated by straight-identified women. Lothian, Busse, and Reid (2007), in their analysis of slash fiction, suggest that "participation in electronic social networks can induct us into new and unusual narratives of identity and sexuality, calling into question familiar identifications and assumptions" (103). Writers and readers of slash fiction, in other words, collectively create space in which women can take a queer turn away from heterofemininity and toward a desire for queer hetero-masculinities.

Lynne Segal (1994) agrees and argues that representations of homoerotic sex between men offer a space where women can be fluid in their gender identifications, sometime being the object of masculine desire and sometimes being the desiring subject while, at the same time, eroticizing the male body as both desiring and penetrable. The recent emergence of "Bend Over Boyfriend" pornography, which features "pegging" or a woman anally penetrating a man with a strap-on dildo, does the same sort of cultural work in terms of eroticizing queer and penetrable hetero-masculinities. Writing and consuming erotica in which two heterosexual men have sex with each other opens narrative space for heterosexually identified women to reimagine both their own sexual subjectivities and ways to eroticize the heteromasculine body.

Like slash fiction and Bend Over Boyfriend, erotic representations and narratives of intimate threesomes that feature two straight men and one woman can do the same sort of cultural work described by Lothian, Busse, and Reid. As I describe above, the heterofeminine erotic habitus could be queered through the eroticization of homoerotic exchanges between two men and a woman in polyqueer threesomes. In threesome narrative or imagery, unlike representations of one-on-one homoerotic interactions between men, a straight woman can imagine herself as the subject and object of masculine desire and as a voyeuristic participant in erotic exchanges between men.

Getting men to take that queer turn, however, is a different matter. Jane Ward's (2008, 2015) research suggests that straight white men actively and concertedly construct their sexual activity with each other as straight by distancing themselves from gay men and deploying raced and classed forms of masculinity that, for them, establish their same-sex activities as part of straight culture. Ward (2008) argues that we need to begin thinking about "queer and straight as cultural spheres that people choose to inhabit in large part because they experience a cultural and political fit" (431).

There is every reason to believe that for some, if not most, straight men, polyqueer WMM threesomes are not an option because they do not resonate with straight culture. However, I wonder if there is something about poly sexualities that include women that differs from the same-sex activities among straight men described by Ward? Might the presence of a woman who is turned on by a WMM threesome offer a bridge from straight culture to queer culture and facilitate a willingness on the part of straight men to take a queer turn?

Agnes Boslo (2012), like Adam Green, is interested in developing a link between the social and erotic desire. Rather than focus on the effects of the broader sexual field as Green does, Boslo narrows her focus to interpersonal dynamics at a micro level. For Boslo, erotic desire between two people is animated by a third element, which is social as well as psychological both in terms of its source and its effects. The third element can be an idealized version of some specific aspect of the desired person taken from more generalizable cultural symbols of attractiveness or sexiness (e.g., large breasts or "washboard" abs) or past experiences with the specific person or someone similar (e.g., *it was hot when I sucked my lover's breasts last time*, or *I've had hot sex with someone with abs similar to this person*").

More important for my purposes here, Boslo also suggests that desire can be animated by being desired by another person (*I want to have sex with this person in this way because it makes me feel desired and that turns me on*) and/or by satisfying a lover (*I want to have sex with this person in this way because it makes them feel turned on and that turns me on*). In other words, the third element that animates erotic desire between two people can be and often is the *thought of a particular partner being turned on.*

Presumably, then, if a heterosexual woman expresses to her partner a strong desire to have a threesome with another man as an erotic experience *for her* (instead of for him), the idea of arousing her could animate her partner's desire to have the experience.[7] This is precisely why I believe that a polyqueer subculture in which participants cultivate narratives and imagery that eroticizes WMM threesomes could open up space for straight men to participate in queer culture (as opposed to the straight culture described by Ward) as straight-identified men. In other words, narratives or imagery that eroticize WMM threesomes—say, an Internet subculture similar to slash fiction—could be a feminist, polyqueer intervention in straight culture.

As is, the hegemonic threesome imaginary is a central feature of straight culture in that it casts WMM threesomes as an aggressive take-turns-on-the-girl scenario in which the woman is objectified, even victimized, or as "gay," which emphasizes the men's desire for each other and renders invisible the woman's desire or subjective experience. Perhaps these cultural narratives about WMM threesomes are more about closing off heterosexual women from eroticizing and desiring a polyqueer threesome involving man-on-man action than they are about men's "natural" competitiveness, jealousy, and explosive reactions. When we consider the popularity of slash fiction, Bend Over Boyfriend pornography, and Oslo's suggestion that heterosexual men's desire can and often is animated by what turns on their partners, perhaps slut-shaming women who desire WMM threesomes is an ideological stopgap to discourage women from expressing this desire lest men acquiesce to turn women on *and like it.*

Same-Gender Loving and Polyqueer Threesomes across Racial Difference

In her book *The Erotic Life of Racism*, Sharon Patricia Holland (2012) asks, "Can work on 'desire' be antiracist work? Can antiracist work *think* desire?" (3). Critical of queer theory's emphasis on desire as liberation, Holland suggests that, in a white supremacist society, desire is always racialized. Racial difference structures the sexual field by laying racialized meaning onto erotic attachments and is embodied as racialized erotic habitus. "It is my contention here that racist practice does limit human desire by attempting to circumscribe its possible attachments. Here I pose that there is no 'raceless' course of desire, and I do so to ascertain the practiced nature of quotidian racism and how those practices shape what we know of as 'desire'" (43).

For Holland, cross-racial touch is a form of quotidian racism in that it "can alter the very idea as well as the actuality of relationships, morphing friends into enemies and strangers into intimates. For touch can encompass empathy as well as violation, passivity as well as active aggression. It can be safely dangerous, or dangerously safe. It also carries a message about the immediate present, the possible future, and the problematic past. Finally, touch crosses boundaries, in fact and imagination" (100). Touch across racial difference, in other words, can be racist to the extent it reproduces racial difference and hierarchies, or it can facilitate interracial identification in ways that dissolve racial hierarchies.

Trimiko Melancon (2014) explores this possibility in *Unbought and Unbossed*. In her provocative and insightful discussion of Ann Allen Shockley's novel *Loving Her*, Melancon suggests that the interracial love affair between Renay, a black woman, and Terry, a white woman, both represents and illustrates the way in which erotic touch and connection across racial difference can at once displace heteronormativity and, at the same time, foster cross-racial identification. For Melancon, Shockley's writing of racial difference as the erotic charge between same-gender-loving women removes gender difference as the eroticized charge and replaces it with non-hierarchical racial difference.

Melancon argues that, rather than writing the racialized other as a sexual object embedded within power relations, Shockley writes racial difference as the eroticized and emotionally intimate bond between the characters that flattens racial hierarchies. In this way, eroticized racial difference stemming from emotional intimacy and not dehumanizing sexual objectification facilitates cross-racial identification without racial "blindness."

> Densely loaded . . . [Shockley's writing] "legitimates" same-sex intimacy and destabilizes (heterosexual) hegemonic notions regarding sexuality. It displaces heterosexuality by foregrounding another paradigm of sexual longing and erotic desire. Emphasizing the "pigmentative" qualities of Renay's and Terry's skin—Renay's golden brownness and Terry's whiteness—the narrator reiterates the interracial-ness and (racial) difference between them (Renay's black body alongside Terry's white body); yet, it locates their sameness—asserting their breasts were like "twins," signifying their commonness. . . . The narrator establishes, at once, their sameness and difference within the context of Renay and Terry's interracial same-sex union. Moreover, its emphasis on the (sexual) converging of black and white female bodies that have historically been constructed as diametrically oppositional—black and white womanhood(s) as constructed dichotomously and contingent on myths of each other— undermines the history and tensions undergirding the social constructions of both black and white womanhood. (97)

As text, the narration of Renay's and Terry's relationship and erotic interactions rewrites racial difference through same-gender loving across race.

Melancon suggests that experiencing non-hierarchical, same-gender loving across race has radical potential for reconfiguring embodied racialized genders and sexualities.

Renay's and Terry's abilities to transcend race in sexual terms/terrain, as well as the (historical) semiotics of black and white female bodies, exemplify the nexus of memory, meaning, and the body: that is, that once the body "forgets" (or "un-remembers") in its quest for pleasure, it, like Renay's and Terry's bodies, liberates itself from historical memory and reductive social constructions—race, gender, and sexuality—that "police" the body. What matters, as Shockley reveals, is not so much shifting social constructions but, rather, how one('s) (body) feels. (97–98)

Building on Holland's and Melancon's work, I want to suggest that erotic threesomes offer an opportunity to reconfigure the dynamics and symbolic meaning of not simply racial difference, but specifically *racialized genders*.

The relationship between white and black men within the U.S. context of white supremacy and resistance to it has always included contestation over and enforcement of possession of women's bodies. A threesome that includes a white and a black man and a black or white woman in the context of an inter-racial threesome places that history directly in bed. As Holland suggests, erotic touch in this context can unfold in ways that reinscribe racial hierarchies or challenge them. For instance, given white men's historical access to black women's bodies, if the woman is black, the white man could experience the threesome as domination not just of the woman, but also the black man. In contrast, if the woman is white, the white man might experience racial superiority by "hot-wifing" to a black man (see Lewis 2010) or, equally plausible, the black man could experience the threesome as reversing white men's unfettered access to black women while prohibiting cross-racial touch between black men and white women, and thus turning the tables on white supremacy. In all of these instances, interracial touch would be both heterosexual (the men are having sex with the woman, but not each other) and embedded within and constitutive of racial hierarchies.

Is this inevitable? I would argue that *polyqueer* interracial threesomes in which the men have sex with each other and the woman would open up potentialities to not only queer heteromasculinity, but also work against racial hierarchies. Here, Melancon's point about same-gender loving is key. Same-gender loving hinges on emotional intimacy and, when experienced across race, works against social hierarchies on the basis of difference. What might an interracial WMM threesome look like if the men were emotionally intimate and have sex with each other? An example of same-gender loving across race in the context of WMM threesomes can be found in the writing of J. M. Bogino (2009). Bogino offers an erotic narrative of two best friends, Jamie, who is white, and Rassahn, who is black.

The story begins with Rassahn talking about how he "wound up in bed with his friend's girl" (119). As he recounts the encounter, we learn that it was a threesome with Jamie and his girlfriend. Describing other threesomes he had with two women, Rassahan says, "Now that was down. . . . Not as down as with Jamie's girl, though. Maybe it was the taboo element: thou shalt not fuck thy best friend's girl. Jamie was his boy, but Rassahn wasn't dissing him because Jamie was in on it, too. Best of both worlds, don't you know" (119). Over two weeks, Rassahn, Jamie, and Jamie's girl have sex together.

> Despite [Rassahn's] prior experience with three-ways, he found it was dif-
> ferent this time. Rassahn was used to women, but he loved to watch Jamie
> with his girl—watch as she wound herself around Jamie's hard body, or
> climbed on top of his broad chest, or took his long dick into her mouth.
> Rassahn loved watching that most. Jamie's head would arch back, his
> longish blonde hair brushing his shoulders and his blue eyes squeezing
> shut. He'd moan softly when he began to come and, at these moments,
> Rassahn would get so excited that he'd take the girl from behind, making
> love to her with his dick while she made love to Jamie with her mouth.
> (120)

Jamie's girl is a queering presence in that she is a conduit for Rassahn and Jamie's friendship to take an erotic turn.

Like Marco Vassi, Bogino writes this erotic interaction in ways that disrupt heteromasculine sexual subjectivity and the gender structure to sexual scripts through a WMM threesome. Rassahn is the desiring subject as he watches Jamie and his girl. He "makes love to her" while she "makes love to Jamie."

In this narrative, it is the woman who encourages the men to make love with each other. "'Why don't you touch him back?' Jamie's girl whispered to him once. He'd shaken his head, but she took his hand. 'Just touch him, that's all. Look at him. He's beautiful . . .'" As Rassahn touches Jamie's chest and moves his hand through "fine golden hairs" and down to where "the hair was thicker, darker, like a field of fresh grass." As Jamie moans, Rassahn is taken over by desire and rolls over. "He closed his eyes and, a second later, somebody's lips were on him" (120).

Significantly, we don't know the race of the woman. By referring to her as "Jamie's girl," and not stating her race, but at the same time, writing her sexual subjectivity as the conduit for the erotic exchange between the two men, Bogino encourages the reader to allow racial identification to recede. Neither man can be read as having a racialized claim to the woman's body, and instead, the reader is invited to focus on the friendship intimacy between Rassahn and Jamie.

Later in the narrative, Rassahn and Jamie find themselves alone watching a baseball game. Without Jamie's girl there, Rassahn feels uncomfortable. "Rassahn hesitated. It felt strange to be alone with Jamie and he realized he hadn't been, not since before that night [they had their first threesome together]. . . . Rassahn hovered on the threshold, wondering what was the matter with him. Jamie was his best friend. That hadn't changed" (121).

After a few beers, Jamie takes Rassahn's hand. "Jamie's middle finger was gently brushing over the ridges on the back of Rassahn's hand. Soft touches, like he gave when they were in bed. Whisper touches that Rassahn could feel in every nerve ending in his body." Rassahn looks down at their hands. "His lay on the couch, nut brown against the beige upholstery, and Jamie's skin was light, pinkish against it. Rassahn's fingers were short and wide, Jamie's long and limber. Small splatters of paint decorated both sets of fingers in a rainbow of colors, identifying them as the hands of two artists" (121). Like Shockley, Bogino emphasizes racial difference in the description of two bodies, but that difference is within the context of similarity. Both Rassahn and Jamie are artists, and because of paint splatter, their hands are "colored" the same. This touch across race is not written as reinforcing a power hierarchy, but instead as making a connection among equals.

Bogino also writes racial difference through the ways in which Jamie and Rassahn speak and what they say. When Jamie kisses him, Rassahn angrily says, "'Don't you *never* kiss me! That shit is *gross!*'" Jamie responds, "'Why're you freaking out? It's not like I haven't done it before.'" Rassahn insists, "'You ain't.'" Jamie points out the obvious. "'I have. . . . My mouth has been all over you, man. What's the problem all of a sudden?'" Rassahn says, "'There was *three* of us them other times . . . .'" Jamie says, "'Just because my girlfriend was there doesn't mean that I wasn't.'" When the two friends discuss what it all means, Rassahn says, "'You know I ain't gay. . . . Look, I don't wanna hurt your feelins or nothing, but . . . shit, man! It's *different* when we all together, you know?'" (122–123). Again, racial difference is present, but racial hierarchy is collapsed through Jamie's vulnerability and Rassahn's rejection.

Eventually, Rassahn leaves, but as he is walking away he reflects on what has happened. "Jamie was his friend, the best he'd ever had, but that didn't mean he was queer for him. Just because he liked hanging out with Jamie more than anybody he'd ever known, just because he liked and trusted Jamie more than anyone in the world, just because the sight of Jamie walking up the street toward him was enough to make his heart sing. . . . Just because sex with Jamie was the best he'd ever had . . ." (123). In Bogino's narrative, the threesome between Jamie, Rassahn, and Jamie's girlfriend is the bridge that opens up the erotic potential for same-gender loving in Jamie's and Rassahn's friendship. Not only is heteromasculinity queered, racial difference is at once present, but racial hierarchy dissolves through erotic touch.

In her research on sex between straight men, Jane Ward (2008) found that when white men discussed sex with black men, "cross-racial sex was permeated with difference and inequality" (428). Sexual encounters across race, in other words, often punctuated race hierarchies rather than dissolved them. Here I am arguing that representations of poly-qeer threesomes that include two straight men of differing races and a woman could offer a counternarrative to those of the straight men described by Ward. Moreover, as I suggested above, perhaps polyqueer narratives of threesomes across race could offer both a feminist intervention in straight culture and an anti-racist intervention in the racial hierarchies that structure straight culture.

In his analysis of James Baldwin's *Another Country*, Matt Brim (2014) offers an insightful critique of the gay character Eric. According to Brim, the gay man, as embodied by Eric, is offered up as a vehicle through which cross-racial identification between straight men is possible through sexual union.

> For is straight male-male sex between black and white men not what Baldwin is really after here? But how to have these men come together lovingly, sexually, in a revelatory experience, without one of them being gay. That story seems to be nowhere in modern literature. This absent story becomes for Baldwin, a—perhaps *the*—question of race. But the goal of racial union is not compelling enough, in a racist, sexist, heter-onormative society, to legitimate sex between straight black and white men. Re-shaped as all the other relationships and identities in the novel may be, that relationship is never "re/disfigured." So Baldwin's novel insists—indeed, must insist—that a gay man occupy one of the straight male positions as men come together to work toward racial union. To put it another way, the gay man takes the pressure off of the straight men, who would otherwise be forced to come together, lovingly, on their own. Of course, they do not, and even in the Baldwin's brilliant queer imagina-

tion, they cannot. Straight male-male sexual love remains an abstraction, unformulated, *queerer than it is possible to say.* (121)

There is, I believe, a monormative presumption here in that Brim can't imagine anything but one-on-one sex between straight men. Bogino's story suggests otherwise. Placing a woman in the sexual interaction opens up narrative space for white and black straight men to experience cross-racial union through erotic interaction and same-gender loving. The presence of the woman places each man on a straight path, but the presence of each other can introduce a queer turn in their erotic orientations.

To the extent that the threesome imaginary is racialized as well as gendered, perhaps representations or embodied experiences of interracial threesomes that are at once intimate and non-hierarchical and that flatten racialized power dynamics rather than punctuate them could facilitate cross-racial identifications. To quote Holland again, "Can work on 'desire' be antiracist work? Can antiracist work *think* desire?" (3). Perhaps the subjective desire for, experience of, and narratives concerning intimate, interracial threesomes that facilitate same-gender loving between straight men constitute and can be productive of not just a queer, feminist desire, but also an anti-racist desire.

Conclusion

Polyamory and the Containment of Polyqueer Sexualities

In this book, I have made an effort to shift feminist, queer, and critical race theory away from the effects of monogamy on individuals within intimate relationships and toward the social and cultural effects of mononormativity and compulsory monogamy in broader social relations and structures of gender and race inequalities. To support this theoretical point, I have explored how narratives of cheating wives and husbands, the social construction of the "black man on the down low," and representations of erotic triangulation in the form of male rivalry and the threesome imaginary rely upon mononormativity and compulsory monogamy to perpetuate racialized notions of masculinities and femininities as well as legitimate hierarchical relationships among and between them.

I have also argued that there is an eminent potential for polyqueer sex and relationships to alter straight lines of heteronormativity, masculine dominance, and racial identification and hierarchies in a very particular way, namely through plurality. By way of example, I tried to illustrate how polyqueer sexualities, relationships, and narratives offer opportunities or potentialities to disrupt not just mononormativity, but also gendered and racialized subjectivities and power relations.

My hope is that an exclusive focus on WMM triangulation provides theoretical clarity, but I am also well aware that it leaves many unanswered questions. For instance, what is the feminist and queer potential of MWW triangulation? What would a polyqueer Vee or threesome look like when the MWW relationship structure and threesome imaginary is ideologically in accordance with hegemonic gender relations? I have focused on the effects on masculinities and only skimmed the surface of femininities. How might polyqueer sexualities transfigure femininities across and within race? How would interracial threesomes differ when two women of different races have a threesome with a man? How do polyqueer sexualities differ depending on the gender and sexual orientations of those involved? How does race intersect with sexual orientation in polyqueer relationships? Is it possible for monogamous couples to queer their relationships or erotic lives with polyqueer sensibilities? What are the obstacles and barriers for some groups in terms of class, race, ethnicity, religion, age, and ability or for all of us when it comes to polyqueer potentialities? Perhaps most important, what are the limits to polyqueer sexualities in terms of structural, interpersonal, and individual transformation, and how might we coordinate polyqueer sexualities with other efforts and strategies for social change and social justice?

Though my focus on WMM sex and relationships is quite narrow and leaves many questions unanswered, my theoretical point is broad. It is that mononormativity is a foundational discourse of relationship morality and health, and dyadic monogamy is assumed to be the only legitimate and fulfilling way to do sexual intimacy and thus is the brass ring of a "good life." As such, mononormativity is a central pillar of contemporary gender, race, class, and sexual relations. It operates at all levels of social organization from the makeup of the self to establishing norms and scripts for our interpersonal interactions and relationships, to structuring our social institutions on a local and national level, to legitimating political, economic, and military domination on a global scale.

Obviously, it is not the only social scaffolding of inequality, but it is an institutionalized system that, in accordance with gender, race, class, and sexuality, has its own logic and structures that obscure, legitimate, and support contemporary power relations. In this book, I have shown that it does so in five specific ways. First, through its own ideological, interpersonal, and structural specificities, mononormativity perpetuates hegemonic constructions of masculinity and femininity and obscures contemporary forms of gender inequality in ostensibly "pure" relationships. Second, within the context of informal but persistent race and class endogamy and to the extent that monogamy closes off the possibility of forging caring and intimate relationships with others, it inhibits cross-class and interracial identification and intimacies. Third, the idea of finding "the one and only" and staking a claim of ownership on another person is not only gendered and racialized, it also reflects and maintains capitalist ideology and the inevitability and desirability of private property. Fourth, mononormativity is deployed as a narrative of cultural difference to legitimate local, national, and global relations of domination along the lines of nation, race, ethnicity, and religion. Finally, mononormativity renders bisexuality invisible and perpetuates essentialist assumptions about sexual orientation and desire. In sum, within the context of Western societies, heteronormative monogamy—as monogamy—includes a well-established and entrenched set of norms, values, scripts, and policies that reflect and sustain power relations that have historically worked in the interests of white, European and American, Christian, class-privileged, heterosexual men.

I have also suggested that mononormativity closes off non-dyadic sex and relationships as a viable option because plural sex and relationships open up potentialities for doing things differently. I focused on polyamory as a subculture and a relationship form that emphasizes gender egalitarianism, non-dyadic bonds of sexual and emotional intimacy, and interpersonal responsibility and accountability to partners and metamours regardless of gender. Polyamory as a subculture and relationship form is in its infancy, and although there are some established norms, it is not like heteronormative monogamy in that it is, as polyamorists often say, DIY. It does not yet have a long-established and entrenched structure and ideology.

This is sociologically and politically important for two reasons. First, as I have tried to argue, the presence of a third or fourth or fifth partner alters power dynamics and opens up the potential to reconfigure our gendered and racialized selves and our interpersonal relationships. Second, while polyamory lacks established and persistent social scaffolding, and this can make the going difficult, it also provides an opportunity to build relationships from the ground up. In my experience, not having a blueprint for relationships handed down from family or community forces my partners and me to be self-reflexive and conscientious about how to make it work and how to do so with a sense of equality and social justice at the fore.

Further, because I often have to explain my relationships to others, not only can I challenge my interlocutors' mononormative assumptions, I can also take the opportunity to challenge their assumptions about gender, race, class, and sexual orientations. As much as I enjoy (and sometimes loathe) those conversations, they can only do so much.

Mononormativity and polyamory matter not just in my life, but also and more importantly, they matter theoretically, sociologically, and politically. My hope is that this book will expand the conversation so that sociologists, as well as queer, feminist, and critical race theorists participate in it. In that spirit, I offer what I hope to be the beginnings of a sociological conceptual apparatus with which feminist, queer, and critical race theorists, sociologists, and polyamorists themselves might distinguish mono- and polynormative sex and relationships from poly-queer ones.

In other words, we're here. We're polyqueer. Let's talk about it.

NOTES

1 Since Rich's foundational work on compulsory heterosexuality, a liberal lesbian and gay rights movement has increased lesbian and gay visibility, expanded access to many of the rights of citizenship once denied same-sex couples, and destigmatized same-sex relationships in ways Adrienne Rich could not have imagined when she wrote the essay. At the same time, women's movements and changes in the economy have led to more economic independence for at least some women and eliminated the option of complete dependence on men's wages for most women. In other words, circulating discourses about relationships, marriage, and gender have changed so that, in the contemporary Western context, the *ideal marriage* is no longer the compulsory, male-dominant patriarchal family described by Rich, but is instead the voluntary *pure relationship* based on the partners' mutual satisfaction and compatibility as equals. Though material inequalities on the basis of gender, race, class, and sexuality are still prevalent within and result from heterosexual marriage, the *discursively constructed* new ideal for marriage no longer does the ideological and compulsory work to subordinate women as a group to men in the ways described by Rich. While the pure relationship ideal is heterosexist and certainly privileges and idealizes heterosexual couples, I would argue that it no longer compels or forces all women into exploitive and unequal relationships with men. I want to suggest that, while the heterosexual, patriarchal marriage no longer does the ideological and economic work to subordinate women to men, the discursive construction of the ideal pure relationship—the monogamous couple—maintains and legitimizes hegemonic gender relations, not just through heteronormativity, but also through *mononormativity* and *compulsory monogamy*.

2 For a description of this shift, see Seidman (1993).

3 Foucault has also been criticized for omitting an analysis of gender. While I agree with much of this criticism, these critiques, unlike critical race theory and queer of color critiques, are not central to my theoretical framework in this book. For a thorough discussion of feminist perspectives on Foucault, see Diamond and Quimby (1988).

4 In this statement, I am excluding the growing body of work specifically on non-monogamies that suggest the queer potential of open and polyamorous relationships. This important work is marginalized in queer theory and sexuality

studies as academic disciplines. Also, while the authors engaged in this work suggest the queer potential of non-monogamies, few develop a coherent theoretical framework for identifying just how non-monogamies might queer gender, sexuality, and race. See, for instance, Rambukkana (2010).

5 For a discussion contrasting the ethics of polygyny and polyamory, see Strauss (2012).

6 An open relationship is one in which the partners agree that sex with others outside the dyad is permissible as long as partners are "faithful" in terms of emotional intimacy. The distinction between open and polyamorous relationships is a false dichotomy in the lived experience of polyamory. Not all open relationships require emotional fidelity. Those would be open polyamorous relationships and are distinguished from what polyamorists call polyfidelity. In the first case, emotional intimacy and commitment are permissible among multiple partners and consensual sexual relations with others outside of the relationship is allowed. Polyfidelity refers to polyamorous relationships in which the partners agree that sex with others outside of the relationships is not permissible.

7 While one study suggests that the majority of polyamorists would be open to multipartner marriage if it were legal, most polyamorists are not politically motivated by or actively seeking legal multipartner marriage (Fleckstein, Bergstrand, and Cox 2012).

8 For a theoretical framework linking class and capitalism to mononormativity, see Klesse (2014).

9 I capitalize "The Monogamous Couple" here and at points elsewhere to emphasize and remind readers that I am referring to an ideal rather than actual monogamous couples or monogamy as it plays out in the lives of individuals. For similar reasons, I also capitalize "The Black Man on the DL" at various points.

10 Researchers rarely ask research participants about desire or how sex feels (with notable exceptions, especially Debra Tolman's [2002] work on adolescent girls' desire), let alone conduct ethnographic studies of threesomes or group sex (again, a notable exception is the work of Katherine Frank [2013]).

11 See, e.g., Anapol (2010) and Taormino (2008).

12 Triangulation and polyamory that include gay, lesbian, transgender, and/or asexual individuals or relationships are certainly queer, not just in terms of heteronormativity, but also in terms of mononormativity. Long before polyamory emerged as a relationship subculture, gay men's sexual subcultures have included norms or at least tolerance of open relationships in which partners are free to have sex with others outside of the couple relationship (see Coelho 2011). Similarly, lesbian feminists have politicized monogamy and advocated polyamory as a specifically transgressive form of woman-centric relating (see Munson and Stelboum 1999). There is also compelling theoretical and empirical work on the benefits of polyamory in terms of transgender identity (Richards 2010) and asexuality (Scherrer 2010).

13 Perhaps, in this regard, it is ironic that I am building on Rich's focus on lesbian existence by claiming polyqueer existence, but my focus is on woman-man-man (WMM), not man-woman-woman (MWW) triangulation. I am therefore open to criticism for excluding lesbian desire and relationships. As Terry Castle (1993) suggests, both Girard and Sedgwick ignore MWW triangulation, thereby rendering invisible lesbian desire and its potential to subvert male dominance. In many ways, I do the same here. However, as I will argue later, a polyamorous resolution to MWW triangulation holds a quite different place in the cultural imaginary of non-monogamy. For Castle, a dyadic resolution in which one of the women marries the man subverts the feminist potential of lesbian bonding. In contrast, both women rejecting the man to form a lesbian couple subverts male dominance. In other words, the feminist potential lies in a dyadic lesbian relationship, not a polyamorous one. The acceptance of a cisgender heterosexual man into a lesbian relationship has far different (hegemonic?) effects than the introduction of a cisgender heterosexual man into a heterosexual relationship. Having said this, there is no doubt that MWW polyamory and erotic interactions have the potential to queer heterofemininity and undermine masculine privilege and power.

CHAPTER 1. MAN AGAINST MAN

1 In contemporary U.S. culture, an active, always-present, and unwavering desire to, not only have sex with women, but also dominate them sexually, is a central feature of hegemonic masculinity (Kimmel 2008; Pascoe 2007). That is, men are portrayed as and assumed to have a compulsive heterosexual desire and hetero-sexual relations are often portrayed or constructed as a relationship of domination and submission regardless of how individual men and women experience heterosex or the existence of subcultural narratives of heterosex that challenge male dominance. While there are other features of hegemonic mascu-linity that are not specific to (though perhaps consistent with) heterosexual desire, such as the use of physical violence to gain status or authority, my focus in this book is specifically on the relationship between masculine-compulsive and -dominant heterosexual desire and feminine sexual objectification and subordi-nation. For this reason, I use the terms "heteromasculinity" and "heterofemininity" to refer to this specific aspect of hegemonic gender relations.
2 Danielle Hidalgo et al. (2008) offer the *dyadic imaginary* as the driver to the fight for marriage equality. They suggest that the desire for marriage rights by gay men and lesbians reflects and maintains the socially constructed image of the couple as the key to happiness and full citizenship. The dyadic imaginary, I would argue, goes far deeper in that it is the relational form that naturalizes the heterosexual relationship between masculinity and femininity.
3 Building on the work of Claude Lévi-Strauss, Gayle Rubin suggests that the function of gender difference in preindustrial societies was to create two different

kinds of people who need each other. Men and women had different skills and duties in the division of labor, which necessitated marriage. The purpose of marriage was not to get men and women together, but instead to form kinship bonds between groups through the exchange of women. According to Rubin, gender socialization and difference served as an institutionalized system to create the need for marriage, thereby facilitating kinship bonds. In the contemporary U.S. world of *pure relationships*, however, the gender division of labor is not what drives marriage; emotional intimacy and physical desire between equals does. In this context, marriage does not require or naturalize gender difference. In contemporary American society, however, mononormativity continues to reinforce the gender binary by insisting that one and only one person will fulfill all of our needs. See Rubin (1975).

4   The social construction of non-Western cultures in anthropological and political discourse as primitive, immoral, and backward relied and continues to rely upon the juxtaposition between polygamous and monogamous marriage. My focus here, however, is specifically the social construction of whiteness through the institutionalized and discursive exclusion of African American kinship from the monogamous couple as a mechanism of racial formation in the United States. For a discussion of monogamy as a colonial discourse, see Willey (2006).

5   As I suggested in my theory of hegemonic masculinity and femininity, when women refuse to play the subordinate complement to hegemonic masculinity, they are cast out as pariahs. At the time I wrote that article, the examples of *pariah femininities* I provided included the slut, bitch, dyke, and prude. All are labels placed on women who refuse to embody the inferior and subordinate role of desirable sexual object in relationship to the desiring masculine subject. Here, I am adding the treacherous, cheating woman to the list.

6   Importantly, this doesn't mean that every heterosexual man wants to consciously possess the woman he loves. It means that masculinity, as a set of ideals for how men should be, includes having control and/or possession of a prized feminine sexual object. No matter how an individual man feels about his relationship with a woman, he is judged and his social status depends on his ability to "keep" her, and so we believe it's *natural* for a man to react as Ben did.

7   An open marriage is one in which partners agree that sexual intimacy with others outside of the couple is permissible.

8   Perhaps the cultural shift in attention from the cheating wife to the rivalry between husband and lover is an ideological mechanism to erase the woman's desire and agency, and bring the focus back to the relationship between the men as desiring subjects. She becomes an object of exchange between the men rather than a desiring and active subject. By casting her as a social pariah and as an object of exchange, this discursive frame for the cheating woman neutralizes the challenge that her desire for two men poses to normative assumptions about

feminine desire and agency, or she is cast as a "slut"—a pariah and outside of normative femininities.

9 In all of my descriptions of my own experiences, the names of others have been changed.

10 The book was on the *New York Times* bestseller list in both hardcover and paperback and won several book awards outside of the academic discipline of anthropology.

11 See, e.g., Saxon (2012).

12 There is certainly an available social script for best friends having sex with the same woman and bonding over their shared experience. When this happens, my theory would predict that there would be a concerted effort by the men to completely reduce the woman to a sexual object void of sexual subjectivity to avoid identification with her as a desiring subject in relationship to each other. As I will discuss later, Sedgwick and others would argue that the exchange of the same woman as an object of desire is a way to heterosexualize homoerotic impulses and desires between straight-identified men (see chapters 3 and 4). When, however, one of the best friends is already partnered with a woman, total objectification is neither possible nor desirable. Therefore, I argue, mononormativity demands that the men become rivals (thereby reducing the possibility of identification) or eliminate the woman from their shared social world.

13 The reader should not assume that the sex represented and implied in this story is more irresponsible or unsafe in terms of sexually transmitted infections than one-on-one sex within the context of a monogamous relationship. In the narrative, Ben, Matthew, and I are what polyamorists call "fluid bonded," meaning we exchange bodily fluids with each other but do not with lovers outside of our relationship. For a discussion of the false assumptions that monogamy is always safe and consensual non-monogamies are always dangerous, see Conley et al. (2013).

CHAPTER 2. BLACK RESPECTABILITY IN A PERFECT WORLD

1 For a cultural history and critique of the emergence of this label, see Boykin (2005).

2 The book is based not on systematic research, but instead on a personal experience with having been cheated on by a man "on the DL" and talking to other women who have had similar experiences.

3 Elsewhere, I argue that there are race-, ethnicity-, and class-specific forms of hegemonic masculinity and femininity in which the characteristics expected of or associated with men within the group are situated as superior and dominant in relationship to feminine characteristics specific to the group. In this case, the respectable man, as head of household, is situated as dominant in relationship to the respectable woman which is the selfless, supportive, and economically dependent role in the African American family. See Schippers (2007).

4 Caroline Pedwell (2008) suggests that we "weave relational webs" as a method for intersectional analyses. Critical of the us/them binary constructed by feminist theorists, researchers, and activists in their construction of the "Western Feminist" and "Third World Woman," Pedwell insists we identify a web of relationships that include, not two identity groups, but instead, the social relationships and resulting power dynamics that result from the social construction of a web of binary relations.

5 It is entirely possible that this is already the case, and rather than MSWM keeping their desires for and relationships with men secret from their partners, perhaps the politics of respectability force African American women and men who are in polyqueer relationships into secrecy. This might explain why, as discussed in the introduction, polyamorous groups and communities, as well as research participants are overwhelmingly middle-class white people.

6 In the single descriptive interjection in the course of the quoted dialogue, Raymond adds, "I said sternly."

7 As discussed in chapter 1, E. Patrick Johnson (2001) identifies "quare theory" as that which brings black experiences and a race analysis from the margins to the center of queer theorizing.

CHAPTER 3. BETWEEN (POLYAMOROUS) MEN

1 Clearly these characters reflect ethnic stereotypes of the rational Brit and the passionate Latin lover. While my focus here is on how gender is queered through polyqueer narrative, I would argue that both class and ethnic difference are queered as well in this film. However, it is beyond the scope of this chapter to unpack how.

2 Pepper Mint (2004) is critical of readers who interpret *Design for Living* as an example of disappearing homosexual desire, and instead suggests reading it as a poly narrative. I clearly agree, and have always read *Design for Living* as a polyamorous text.

3 I would like to especially thank Lisa Wade for suggesting this as an alternative ending to the film.

CHAPTER 4. THE HETEROMASCULINE BODY AND THE THREESOME IMAGINARY

1 For a thorough anthropological and historical discussion of group sex across time and cultures, see Frank (2013).

2 I found three explanations for this label. One is that the devil was known to have a forked penis and could simultaneously penetrate a woman vaginally and anally. The second is that a WMM threesome involves two "horns," just like the devil. The third is that "normal" threesomes are MWW and WMM threesomes are "evil," "wrong," or "bad." The online Urban Dictionary distinguishes the "devil's threesome" from a "love sandwich," which refers to a MWW threesome. I would

argue that, regardless of the origin of these labels, the negative connotation of WMM threesomes and the positive connotation of MWW threesomes is reflected in and perpetuated by these labels. See "Devil's Three-Way" (n.d.).

3 Katherine Frank, personal Facebook correspondence, and Ryan Scoats, personal email correspondence.

4 Ryan Scoats, personal email correspondence.

5 There are, of course, exceptions where men engage in WMM threesomes or group sex that includes one woman and two or more men. Gangbangs or group sex in which two or more men "take turns" on a woman is a readily available component of the heteromasculine imaginary and not an uncommon bonding ritual among men. In her extensive review of anthropological and sociological research on group sex, Katherine Frank (2013) suggests that gangbangs are more about establishing and maintaining bonds and status hierarchies among men than expressing a repressed homoerotic desire for each other.

> When group sex occurs among an apparently heterosexual group of men and a woman, the scenarios are often termed "homoerotic." Sharing the body of a woman (or women) is believed to be arousing because it draws erotic power from feelings the men have for each other but cannot express directly. But while unacknowledged same-sex desires might exist, it would be a mistake to overlook the other processes and attachments involved. (236)

Interestingly, Frank suggests that, although these exchanges are heterosexualized by ideologically and interactively situating the men as in control and desiring subjects in relationship to the woman's body as an object, the labels "heterosexual" and "homosexual" are blurred in a way that would not be the case in dyadic sex. In other words, the social construction of gangbangs as "taking turns on the woman" through porn, myth, and strict norms for doing masculinity in the context of a gangbang orient group sex on the straight line of heteromasculinity.

This is also the case with the game of "hot-wifing." Significantly, there are often strict prohibitions against physical contact between the husband and the other man. In this role play, the husband is in control in terms of the gaze (he watches rather than participates, so, in a way much like the threesome with two women, he is the desiring and gazing subject and the "action" is for him). The husband who desires this erotic interaction experiences it as an exchange between himself and the man having sex with his wife. A central component to this erotic game is the husband "reclaiming" his wife by having sex with her after the other man does. Again, the rules of the game heterosexualize WMM sex by prohibiting contact between the men and situating the wife as the object in their exchange. And as is the case in gangbangs, the rules and ideological construction of what the participants are doing and its meaning go a long way to heterosexualize what is or could be a rather homoerotic interaction between the men.

6   Individuals who identify as asexual would probably not desire or seek erotic destruction.

7   This could especially be the case during the phase of a relationship that involves what polyamorists call "new relationship energy" (NRE). NRE refers to the euphoric feeling when one becomes involved with and begins building intimacy with a new lover. Polyamorists have a language for this phase of a relationship because when experiencing NRE with a new partner, it is easy to neglect existing relationships. While polyamorists warn of the effects of NRE, perhaps it offers a window of opportunity for heterosexual women to introduce WMM threesomes as a strong desire.

BIBLIOGRAPHY

Adam, Barry. 2006. "Relationship Innovation in Male Couples." *Sexualities* 9(1): 5–26.

Ahmed, Sara. 2007. *Queer Phenomenology: Orientations, Objects, Others.* Durham, NC: Duke University Press.

Al-Zubi, Hasan. 2004. "Sexual Fantasies in J. K. Huysmans's *Against the Grain* and Leopoldo Alas's *Regenta*." *Journal of Bisexuality* 4(3–4): 7–27.

Anapol, Deborah. 2004. "A Glimpse of Harmony." *Journal of Bisexuality* 4(3–4): 109–119.

Anapol, Deborah. 2010. *Polyamory in the 21st Century: Love and Intimacy with Multiple Partners.* New York: Rowman & Littlefield.

Anderlini-D'Onofrio, Serena. 2004a. "Plural Loves: Bi and Poly Utopias for a New Millennium." *Journal of Bisexuality* 4(3–4): 1–6.

Anderlini-D'Onofrio, Serena. 2004b. "Sacred Bi Love." *Journal of Bisexuality* 4(3–4): 199–218.

Anderlini-D'Onofrio, Serena. 2009. "Plural Happiness: Bi and Poly Triangulations in Balasko's *French Twist*." *Journal of Bisexuality* 9(3–4): 343–361.

Anderson, Eric. 2014. *21st-Century Jocks.* Basingstoke: Palgrave Macmillan.

Balasubramanian, Janani. 2013. "9 Strategies for Non-Oppressive Polyamory." *Black Girl Dangerous (BGD)*, October 4. http://www.blackgirldangerous. org/2013/10/9-strategies-for-oppressive-polyamory/.

Bard, Taliesin. 2004. "Just Like a Hollywood Movie." *Journal of Bisexuality* 4(3–4): 177–198.

Barker, Meg. 2005. "This Is My Partner, and This Is My . . . Partner's Partner: Constructing a Polyamorous Identity in a Monogamous World." *Journal of Constructivist Psychology* 18(1): 75–88.

Barker, Meg. 2013. *Rewriting the Rules: An Integrative Guide to Love, Sex and Relationships.* New York: Routledge.

Barker, Meg, and Darren Langdridge (Eds.). 2010a. *Understanding Non-Monogamies.* New York: Routledge.

Barker, Meg, and Darren Langdridge. 2010b. "Whatever Happened to Non-Monogamies? Critical Reflections on Recent Research and Theory." *Sexualities* 13(6): 748–772.

Bauer, Robin. 2010. "Non-Monogamy in Queer BDSM Communities: Putting the Sex Back into Alternative Relationship Practices and Discourse." In Meg Barker and Darren Langdridge (Eds.), *Understanding Non-Monogamies.* New York: Routledge.

Bell, David. 2006. "Bodies, Technologies, Spaces: On 'Dogging.'" *Sexualities* 9(4): 387–407.

Bell, Alan, and Martin Weinberg. 1978. *Homosexualities: A Study of Diversity among Men and Women*. New York: Simon & Schuster.

Black & Poly. n.d. *Meetup*. http://www.meetup.com/Black-Poly-NYC/.

Blasband, David ,and Letitia Peplau. 1985. "Sexual Exclusivity versus Openness in Gay Male Couples." *Archives of Sexual Behavior* 14(5): 395–412.

Block, Jenny. 2008. *Open: Love, Sex, and Life in an Open Marriage*. Berkeley, CA: Seal Press.

Blumenfield, Tami. 2009. "The Na of Southwest China: Debunking the Myths." *Portland State University*, May. Originally at http://web.pdx.edu/~tblu2/na.html. Archived at https://web.archive.org/web/20110720025007/http://web.pdx.edu/~tblu2/Na/myths.pdf.

Blumstein, Philip, and Pepper Schwartz. 1983. *American Couples*. New York: William Morrow.

Bogino, J. M. 2009. "Threshold." In R. Jackson (Ed.), *Bi Guys: The Deliciousness of His Sex*. Maple Shade, NJ: Lethe Press.

Boslo, Agnes. 2012. "Sociological Discipline and the Unruly Erotic." *Review of European Studies* 4(1): 94–106.

Boykin, Keith. 2005. *Beyond the Down Low: Sex, Lies, and Denial in Black America*. New York: Carroll and Graf.

Branfman, Jonathan, and Susan Ekberg Stiritz. 2012. "Teaching Men's Anal Pleasure: Challenging Gender Norms with 'Prostage' Education." *American Journal of Sexuality Education* 7(4): 404–428.

Breen, Margaret Soenser. 2001. "Radclyffe Hall, E. Lynn Harris, and Franz Kafka: Christianity, Queerness, and the Politics of Normalcy." *International Journal of Sexuality and Gender Studies* 6(4): 293–304.

Brim, Matt. 2014. *James Baldwin and the Queer Imagination*. Ann Arbor: University of Michigan Press.

Brown, Arch. 2005. "To Fuck and Be Fucked." *Journal of Bisexuality* 5(2–3): 171–177.

Brown, Rodney McGruder. 2014. "Say It Loud: I Am a Black Bisexual Male and I'm Proud." In Robyn Ochs and H. Sharif Williams (Eds.), *Recognize: The Voices of Bisexual Men*. Boston: Bisexual Resource Center.

Bryant, Carl, and Salvador Vidal-Ortiz. 2008. "Introduction to Retheorizing Homophobias." *Sexualities* 11(4): 387–396.

Bryant, Wayne M. 2004. "Bi Film-Video World: Bi Poly Cinema." *Journal of Bisexuality* 4(3–4): 219–226.

Butler, Judith. 1990. *Gender Trouble: Feminism and the Subversion of Identity*. New York: Routledge.

Cardoso, Daniel, Carla Correia, and Danielle Capella. 2009. "Polyamory as a Possibility of Feminine Empowerment." Paper presented at the Ninth Congress of the Euro-

pean Sociological Association, Lisbon, Portugal, September. http://www.academia.
edu/564397/Polyamory_as_a_possibility_of_feminine_empowerment.

Cascais, Antonio Fernando, and Daniel Cardoso, 2012. "'Loving Many': Polyamorous Love, Gender and Identity." In Naomi de Haro García and Maria-Anna
Tseliou (Eds.), *Gender and Love: Interdisciplinary Perspectives*, 2d ed. Ebook:
Inter-Disciplinary Press. http://www.inter-disciplinary.net/publishing/product/
gender-and-love-interdisciplinary-perspectives/.

Castle, Terry. 1993. *The Apparitional Lesbian: Female Homosexuality and Modern Culture*. New York: Columbia University Press.

"The Cheating Husband." n.d. *Infidelity & Cheating Information Site*. http://www.
infidelity-help.us.com/section.php/cheating-husband/.

"The Cheating Wife." n.d. *Infidelity & Cheating Information Site*. http://www.infidelity-
help.us.com/section.php/cheating-wife/.

Clum, John. 1994. *Acting Gay: Male Homosexuality in Modern Drama*. New York:
Columbia University Press.

Coelho, Tony. 2011. "Hearts, Groins and the Intricacies of Gay Male Open Relationships: Sexual Desire and Liberation Revisited." *Sexualities* 14(6): 653–668.

Conley, Terri D., Ali Ziegler, Amy C. Moors, Jes L. Matsick, and Brandon Valentine.
2013. "A Critical Examination of Popular Assumptions about the Benefits and
Outcomes of Monogamous Relationships." *Personality and Social Psychology Review*
17(2): 124–141.

Connell, R. W. 2005. *Masculinities*, 2d ed. Berkeley: University of California Press.

Coontz, Stephanie. 2005. *Marriage, a History: How Love Conquered Marriage*. New
York: Penguin Books.

Dean, Terrance. 2010. "The Intern." In Terrance Dean, James Earl Hardy, and Stanley
Bennett Clay, *Visible Lives: Three Stories in Tribute to E. Lynn Harris*. New York:
Kensington.

de Beauvoir, Simone. 1949. *The Second Sex*. New York: Vintage.

de Boer, A., E. M. van Buel, and G. J. Ter Horst. 2012. "Love Is More than Just a Kiss: A
Neurobiological Perspective on Love and Affection." *Neuroscience* 201: 114–124.

Decena, Carlos Ulises. 2008. "Profiles, Compulsory Disclosure and Ethical Sexual
Citizenship in the Contemporary USA." *Sexualities* 11(4): 397–413.

DeMaria, Richard. 1978. *Communal Love at Oneida: A Perfectionist Vision of Authority, Property and Sexual Order*. New York: Edwin Mellen Press."Devil's
Three-Way." n.d. *Urban Dictionary*. http://www.urbandictionary.com/define.
php?term=devil%27s+three-way.

Diamond, Irene, and Lee Quimby (Eds.). 1988. *Feminism and Foucault: Reflections on
Resistance*. Boston: Northeastern University Press.

Easton, Dossie, and Janet W. Hardy. 2009. *The Ethical Slut: A Practical Guide to Polyamory, Open Relationships, and Other Adventures*, 2d ed. Berkeley, CA: Celestial
Arts.

Elia, John P. 2003. "Queering Relationships: Toward a Paradigmatic Shift." *Journal of Homosexuality* 45 (2/3/4): 61–86.

Ellsworth, Ryan. 2011. "The Human That Never Evolved: A Review of Christopher Ryan and Cacilda Jethá, *Sex at Dawn: How We Mate, Why We Stray, and What It Means for Modern Relationships*." *Evolutionary Psychology* 9(3): 325–335.

Fields, Errol L., Laura M. Bogart, Katherine C. Smith, David J. Malebranche, Jonathan Ellen, and Mark A. Schuster. 2012. "HIV Risk and Perceptions of Masculinity Among Young Black Men Who Have Sex with Men." *Journal of Adolescent Health* 50: 296–303.

Fleckstein, Jim, Crutis Bergstrand, and Derrell Cox. 2012. "What Do Polys Want?: An Overview of the 2012 Loving More Survey." *Loving More*.http://www.lovemore.com/polyamory-articles/2012-lovingmore-polyamory-survey/.

Ford, Chandra L., Kathryn D. Whetten, Susan A. Hall, Jay S. Kaufman, and Angela D. Thrasher. 2007. "Black Sexuality, Social Construction, and Research Targeting 'The Down Low' ('The DL')." *Annals of Epidemiology* 17(3): 209–216.

Foucault, Michel. 1978. *History of Sexuality Volume 1: An Introduction*. New York: Vintage.

Frank, Katherine. 2008. "'Not Gay, but Not Homophobic': Male Sexuality and Homophobia in the 'Lifestyle.'" *Sexualities* 11(4): 435–454.

Frank, Katherine. 2013. *Plays Well in Groups: A Journey through the World of Group Sex*. New York: Rowman & Littlefield.

Frank, Katherine, and John DeLamater. 2010. "Deconstructing Monogamy: Boundaries, Identities, and Fluidities across Relationships." In Meg Barker and Darren Langdridge (Eds.), *Understanding Non-Monogamies*. New York: Routledge.

Gammon, Mark A., and Kirsten L. Isgro. 2006. "Troubling the Canon." *Journal of Homosexuality* 52(1–2): 159–184.

Garber, Marjorie. 2000. "Erotic Triangles" and "Threesomes," in *Bisexuality and the Eroticism of Everyday Life*. New York: Routledge.

Giddens, Anthony. 1992. *The Transformation of Intimacy: Sexuality, Love, and Eroticism in Modern Societies*. Oxford: Polity.

Giorno, John. 1994. *You Got to Burn to Shine*. New York: High Risk Books/Serpent's Tail.

Girard, René. 1965. *Deceit, Desire, and the Novel: Self and Other in Literary Structure*. Baltimore: Johns Hopkins University Press.

Green, Adam Isaiah. 2008a. "The Social Organization of Desire: The Sexual Fields Approach." *Sociological Theory* 26(1): 25–50.

Green, Adam Isaiah. 2008b. "Erotic Habitus: Toward a Sociology of Desire." *Theoretical Sociology* 37: 597–626.

Green, Adam Isaiah. 2010. "Remembering Foucault: Queer Theory and Disciplinary Power." *Sexualities* 13(3): 316–337.

Guss, Jeffrey. 2010. "The Danger of Desire: Anal Sex and the Homo/Masculine Subject." *Studies in Gender and Sexuality* 11(3): 124–140.

Halberstam, Judith. 2005. *In a Queer Time and Place: Transgender Bodies, Subcultural Lives* New York: New York University Press.

Hale, C. Jacob. 2002. "Leatherdyke Boys and Their Daddies." In Kim M. Phillips and Barry Reay (Eds.), *Sexualities in History*. New York: Routledge.

Hamilton, Laura, and Elizabeth A. Armstrong. 2009. "Gendered Sexuality in Young Adulthood: Double Binds and Flawed Options." *Gender & Society* 23(5): 589–616.

Hammers, Corie J. 2008. "Making Space for an Agentic Sexuality? The Examination of a Lesbian/Queer Bathhouse." *Sexualities* 11(5): 547–572.

Hammonds, Evelynn M. 1994. "Black (W)holes and the Geometry of Black Female Sexuality." *Differences: A Journal of Feminist Cultural Studies* 6(2–3): 126–145.

Hardy, James Earl. 2010. "Is It Still Jood to Ya?" In Terrance Dean, James Earl Hardy, and Stanley Bennett Clay, *Visible Lives: Three Stories in Tribute to E. Lynn Harris*. New York: Kensington.

Haritaworn, Jin, Chin-ju Lin, and Christian Klesse. 2006. "Poly/logue: A Critical Introduction to Polyamory." *Sexualities* 9(5): 515–529.

Harris, E. Lynn. 1991. *Invisible Life*. New York: Anchor.

Heckert, Jamie. 2010. "Love without Borders? Intimacy, Identity and the State of Compulsory Monogamy." In Meg Barker and Darren Langdridge (Eds.), *Understanding Non-Monogamies*. New York: Routledge.

Heinlein, Robert A. 1961. *Stranger in a Strange Land*. New York: Berkeley Medallion.

Hidalgo, Danielle, Kristen Barber, and Erica Hunter. 2008. "The Dyadic Imaginary: Troubling the Perception of Love as Dyadic." *Journal of Bisexuality* 7(3–4): 171–189.

Higginbotham, Evelyn Brooks. 1993. *Righteous Discontent: The Women's Movement in the Black Baptist Church, 1880–1920*. Cambridge, MA: Harvard University Press.

Hill Collins, Patricia. 2002. *Black Feminist Thought: Knowledge, Consciousness, and the Politics of Empowerment*, 2d ed. New York: Routledge.

Hill Collins, Patricia. 2005. *Black Sexual Politics: African Americans, Gender, and the New Racism*. New York: Routledge.

Ho, Petula Sik Ying. 2006. "The (Charmed) Circle Game: Reflections on Sexual Hierarchy through Multiple Sexual Relationships." *Sexualities* 9(5): 547–564.

Holland, Sharon Patricia. 2012. *The Erotic Life of Racism*. Durham, NC: Duke University Press.

Hoppe, Trevor. 2011. "Circuits of Power, Circuits of Pleasure: Sexual Scripting in Gay Men's Bottom Narratives." *Sexualities* 14(2): 193–217.

Houston, Ruth. 2011. "Why Women Cheat vs. Why Men Cheat—They Cheat for Different Reasons." *Examiner*, April 7. http://www.examiner.com/article/why-women-cheat-vs-why-men-cheat-they-cheat-for-different-reasons.

Iantaffi, Alessandra (Alex). 2010. "Disability and Polyamory: Exploring the Edges of Inter Dependence, Gender and Queer Issues in Non-Monogamous Relationships." In Meg Barker and Darren Langdridge (Eds.), *Understanding Non-Monogamies*. New York: Routledge.

Ingraham, Chrys (Ed.). 2005. *Thinking Straight: The Power, Promise, and Paradox of Heterosexuality*. New York: Routledge.

Jackson, Lisa D. 2012. "Big Lie, Small World: What E. Lynn Harris Wanted Readers to Understand about the Struggle for African American, Homosexual Males Seeking to Attain the American Dream." *Journal of Homosexuality* 59(4): 1095–1112.

Jackson, Stevi, and Sue Scott. 2004. "The Personal Is Still Political: Heterosexuality, Feminism and Monogamy." *Feminism & Psychology* 14(1): 151–157.

Johnson, E. Patrick. 2001. "'Quare' Studies, or (Almost) Everything I Know about Queer Studies I Learned from My Grandmother." *Text and Performance Quarterly* 21(1): 1–25.

Julz. 2005. "Magic Man." *Journal of Bisexuality* 5(2–3): 213–220.

Karlen, Arno. 1988. *Threesomes: Studies in Sex, Power, and Intimacy*. Sag Harbor, NY: Beech Tree Books.

Kern, Louis J. 1981. *An Ordered Love: Sex Roles and Sexuality in Victorian Utopias: The Shakers, the Mormons, and the Oneida Community*. Chapel Hill: University of North Carolina.

Kimmel, Michael. 2008. *Guyland: The Perilous World Where Boys Become Men*. New York: Harper.

King, J. L. (with Karen Hunter). 2004. *On the Down Low: A Journey into the Lives of "Straight" Black Men Who Sleep with Men*. New York: Harlem Moon.

Kipnis, Laura. 2003. *Against Love: A Polemic*. New York: Vintage.

Klesse, Christian. 2006. "Polyamory and Its 'Others': Contesting the Terms of Non-Monogamy." *Sexualities* 9(5): 565–583.

Klesse, Christian. 2010. "Paradoxes in Gender Relations: [Post] Feminism and Bisexual Polyamory." In Meg Barker and Darren Langdridge (Eds.), *Understanding Non-Monogamies*. New York: Routledge.

Klesse, Christian. 2014. "Poly Economics—Capitalism, Class, and Polyamory." *International Journal of Politics, Culture, and Society* 27(2): 203–220.

Klesse, Christian, and Dossie Easton. 2006. "The Trials and Tribulations of Being a 'Slut'—Ethical, Psychological, and Political Thoughts on Polyamory." *Sexualities* 9(5): 643–650.

Konstanza. 2004. "In the Forecourt of Paradise." *Journal of Bisexuality* 4(3–4): 121–132.

Kurdek, Lawrence A., and J. Patrick Schmitt. 1985. "Relationship Quality of Gay Men in Closed or Open Relationships." *Journal of Homosexuality* 12(2): 85–99.

Labriola, Kathy. 2013. *The Jealousy Workbook: Exercises and Insights for Managing Open Relationships*. Greenery Press.

Lamont, Ellen. 2014. "Reconciling Egalitarian Ideals with Traditional Gender Norms." *Gender & Society* 28(2): 189–211.

Lavie-Ajayi, Maya, Colette D. R. Jones, and Lucy Russell. 2010. "Social Sex: Young Women and Early Sexual Relationships." In Meg Barker and Darren Langdridge (Eds.), *Understanding Non-Monogamies*. New York: Routledge.

Lewis, Angela. 2010. "Not without My Wife: An Exploration of the Cuckolding Lifestyle." *Counselling Australia* 10(3): 1–6.

Lind, Gregg. 2005. "Coming Out Swinging." *Journal of Bisexuality* 5(2–3): 163–170.

Lothian, Alexis, Kristina Busse, and Robin Anne Reid. 2007. "'Yearning Void and
Infinite Potential': Online Slash Fandom as Queer Female Space." *English Language
Notes* 45(2): 103–111.

Malebranche, David J. Errol L. Fields, Lawrence O. Bryant, and Shaun R. Harper. 2009.
"Masculine Socialization and Sexual Risk Behaviors among Black Men Who Have
Sex with Men: A Qualitative Exploration." *Men and Masculinities* 12(1): 90–112.

Mandelbaum, David G. 1938. "Polyandry in Kota Society." *American Anthropologist*
40(4): 574–583.

Marie, Joy. 2008. *The Straight-Up Truth about the Down-Low*. n.l.: Creative Wisdom
Books.

Mariposa, Mel. 2013. "Polynormativity and the New Poly Paradigm." *Polysingleish* (blog), February 1. http://polysingleish.com/2013/02/01/
polynormativity-and-the-new-poly-paradigm/.

McBride, Dwight. 2005. *Why I Hate Abercrombie and Fitch: Essays on Race and Sexuality*. New York: New York University Press.

McLean, Kirsten. "Negotiating (Non)Monogamy." *Journal of Bisexuality* 4(1–2): 83–97.

McWhirter, David P., and Andrew M. Mattison. 1984. *The Male Couple: How Relationships Develop*. Englewood Cliffs, NJ: Prentice-Hall.

Melancon, Trimiko. 2014. *Unbought and Unbossed: Transgressive Black Women, Sexuality, and Representation*. Philadelphia: Temple University Press.

Melby, Todd. 2005. "Anal Sex: An Extraordinary Taboo." *Contemporary Sexuality*
41(11): 1–6.

Messner, Michael. 2002. *Taking the Field: Women, Men, and Sports*. Berkeley: University of California Press.

Michael, Robert T., John H. Gagnon, Edward O. Laumann, and Gena Kolata. 1994. *Sex
in America: A Definitive Study*. New York: Little, Brown & Co.

Mint, Pepper. 2004. "The Power Dynamics of Cheating." *Journal of Bisexuality* 4(3–4):
55–76.

Mint, Pepper. 2007. "Polyamory Is Not Necessarily Queer." *Freaksexual* (blog), March 13. https://freaksexual.wordpress.com/2007/03/13/
polyamory-is-not-necessarily-queer/.

Mint, Pepper. 2010. "The Power Mechanisms of Jealousy." In Meg Barker and Darren
Langdridge (Eds.), *Understanding Non-Monogamies*. New York: Routledge.

Mitchell, Melissa, Kim Bartholomew, and Rebecca J. Cobb. 2013. "Need Fulfillment in
Polyamorous Relationships." *Journal of Sex Research* 51(3): 329–339.

Moynihan, Daniel Patrick. 1965. *The Negro Family: The Case for National Action*.
Washington, DC: Office of Policy Planning and Research, United States Department of Labor.

Muncy, Raymond Lee. 1973. *Sex and Marriage in Utopian Communities: 19th-Century America*. Bloomington: Indiana University Press.

Muñoz, José Esteban. 2009. *Cruising Utopia: The Then and There of Queer Futurity*. New York: New York University Press.

Munson, Marcia, and Judith P. Stelboum (Eds.). 1999. *The Lesbian Polyamory Reader: Open Relationships, Non-Monogamy, and Casual Sex*. Binghamton, NY: Haworth Press.

Noël, Melita J. 2006. "Progressive Polyamory: Considering Issues of Diversity." *Sexualities* 9(5): 602–620.

The Other Man. 2008. Richard Eyre (Dir.); Richard Eyre and Charles Wood (Scr.). Chatsworth, CA: Image Entertainment. Film.

Pallotta-Chiarolli, Maria. 1995. "Choosing Not to Choose: Beyond Monogamy, beyond Duality." In Kevin Lano and Claire Parry (Eds.), *Breaking the Barriers to Desire*. London: Five Leaves.

Pallotta-Chiarolli, Maria. 2006. "On the Borders of Sexuality Research: Young People Who Have Sex with Both Males and Females." *Journal of Gay and Lesbian Issues in Education* 3(2/3): 79–86.

Pallotta-Chiarolli, Maria. 2008. *Love You Two*. Sydney: Random House.

Pallotta-Chiarolli, Maria. 2010a. *Border Sexualities, Border Families in Schools*. New York: Rowman & Littlefield.

Pallotta-Chiarolli, Maria. 2010b. "'To Pass, Border or Pollute': Polyfamilies Go to School." In Meg Barker and Darren Langdridge (Eds.), *Understanding Non-Monogamies*. New York: Routledge.

Pallotta-Chiarolli, Maria. 2011. "You're Too Queer for the Straights and Now Too Queer for the Gays!" *Journal of Bisexuality* 11(4): 566–570.

Pallotta-Chiarolli, Maria, and Sara Lubowitz. 2003. "Outside Belonging: Multi-Sexual Relationships as Border Existence." In Serena Anderlini-D'Onofrio (Ed.), *Women and Bisexuality: A Global Perspective*. New York: Haworth Press.

Pallotta-Chiarolli, Maria, and Erik Martin. 2009. "'Which Sexuality? Which Service?' Bisexual Young People's Experiences with Youth, Queer and Mental Health Services." *Journal of LGBT Youth* 6(2/3): 199–222.

Park, Willard Z. 1937. "Paviotso Polyandry." *American Anthropologist* 39(2): 366–368.

Pascoe, C. J. 2007. *Dude, You're a Fag: Masculinity and Sexuality in High School*. Berkeley: University of California Press.

Pedwell, Carolyn. 2008. "Weaving Relational Webs: Theorizing Cultural Difference and Embodied Practice." *Feminist Theory* 9(1): 87–107.

Penley, Constance. 1995. "Feminism, Psychoanalysis, and the Study of Popular Culture." In Lawrence Grossberg (Ed.), *Cultural Studies*. New York: Routledge.

Peplau, L., and S. Cochran. 1981. "Value Orientation in the Intimate Relationships of Gay Men." *Journal of Homosexuality* 6(3): 1–19.

Peter, Leonie, and Ron Owen. 2000. "Forget 2001, It's 20/10 for Us." *Journal of Bisexuality* 1(1): 71–86.

Phillips, Shalanda. 2010. "There Were Three in the Bed: Discursive Desire and the Sex Lives of Swingers." In Meg Barker and Darren Langdridge (Eds.), *Understanding Non-Monogamies*. New York: Routledge.

Pieper, Marianne, and Robin Bauer. 2005. "Call for Papers." International Conference on Polyamory and Mono-Normativity, Research Centre for Feminist, Gender & Queer Studies, University of Hamburg, Germany, November 5–6.

Piercy, Marge. 1985. *A Woman on the Edge of Time*. New York: Fawcett.

Poly People of Color. n.d. *Tumblr*. http://polypeopleofcolor.tumblr.com.

Rambukkana, Nathan. 2004. "Uncomfortable Bridges." *Journal of Bisexuality* 4(3–4): 141–154.

Rambukkana, Nathan. 2010. "Sex, Space and Discourse: Non/Monogamy and Intimate Privilege in the Public Sphere." In Meg Barker and Darren Langdridge (Eds.), *Understanding Non-Monogamies*. New York: Routledge).

Rambukkana, Nathan. 2015. *Fraught Intimacies: Non-Monogamy in the Public Sphere*. Vancouver: UBC Press.

Reid-Pharr, Robert. 2001. *Black Gay Man: Essays*. New York: New York University Press.

Rich, Adrienne. 1983. "Compulsory Heterosexuality and Lesbian Existence." In Ann Snitow, Christine Stansell, and Sharon Thompson (Eds.), *Powers of Desire: The Politics of Sexuality*. New York: Monthly Review Press.

Richards, Christina. 2010. "Trans and Non-Monogamies." In Meg Barker and Darren Langdridge (Eds.), *Understanding Non-Monogamies*. New York: Routledge.

Riggs, Damien W. 2010. "Developing a 'Responsible' Foster Care Praxis: Poly as a Framework for Examining Power and Propriety in Family Contexts." In Meg Barker and Darren Langdridge (Eds.), *Understanding Non-Monogamies*. New York: Routledge.

Ritchie, Ani, and Meg Barker. 2006. "'There Aren't Words for What We Do or How We Feel So We Have to Make Them Up': Constructing Polyamorous Languages in a Culture of Compulsory Monogamy." *Sexualities* 9(5): 584–601.

Robins, Suzann. 2004. "Remembering the Kiss . . ." *Journal of Bisexuality* 4(3–4): 99–108.

Robinson, Margaret. 2013. "Polyamory and Monogamy as Strategic Identities." *Journal of Bisexuality* 13(1): 21–38.

Robinson, Victoria. 1997. "My Baby Just Cares for Me: Feminism, Heterosexuality, and Non-Monogamy." *Journal of Gender Studies* 6(2): 143–158.

Rubin, Gayle. 1975. "The Traffic in Women: Notes on the 'Political Economy' of Sex." In Rayna Reiter (Ed.), *Toward an Anthropology of Women*. New York: Monthly Review Press.

Rubin, Gayle. 1984. "Thinking Sex: Notes for a Radical Theory of the Politics of Sexuality." In Carole S. Vance (Ed.), *Pleasure and Danger: Exploring Female Sexuality*. London: Pandora.

Ryan, Christopher, and Cacilda Jethá. 2010. *Sex at Dawn: The Prehistoric Origins of Modern Sexuality*. New York: Harper.

Sandfort, Theo G. M., and Brian Dodge. 2008. "'. . . And Then There Was the Down Low': Introduction to Black and Latino Male Bisexualities." *Archive of Sexual Behavior* 37: 675–682.

Sartorius, Annina. 2004. "Three and More in Love: Group Marriage or Integrating Commitment and Sexual Freedom." *Journal of Bisexuality* 4(3–4): 79–98.

Saxey, Esther. 2010. "Non-Monogamy and Fiction." In Meg Barker and Darren Langdridge (Eds.), *Understanding Non-Monogamies*. New York: Routledge.

Saxon, Lynn. 2012. *Sex at Dusk: Lifting the Shiny Wrapping off of Sex at Dawn*. n.l.: CreateSpace.

Scherrer, Kristen S. 2010. "Asexual Relationships: What Does Asexuality Have to Do with Polyamory?" In Meg Barker and Darren Langdridge (Eds.), *Understanding Non-Monogamies*. New York: Routledge.

Schilt, Kristen, and Elroi Windsor. 2014. "The Sexual Habitus of Transgender Men: Negotiating Sexuality through Gender." *Journal of Homosexuality* 61(5): 732–748.

Schippers, Mimi. 2002. *Rockin' Out of the Box: Gender Maneuvering in Alternative Hard Rock*. New Brunswick, NJ: Rutgers University Press.

Schippers, Mimi. 2007. "Recovering the Feminine Other: Femininity, Masculinity, and Gender Hegemony." *Theory and Society* 36(1): 85–102.

Schippers, Mimi. 2012. "Third Wave Rebels in a Second Wave World: Polyamory, Gender, and Power." In Donna King and Carrie Smith (Eds.), *Men Who Hate Women and the Women Who Kick Their A@#$!: Feminist Perspectives on the Stieg Larsson Millennium Trilogy*. Nashville, TN: Vanderbilt University Press.

Scoats, Ryan, Lauren J. Joseph, and Eric Anderson. Forthcoming. "Two Men, One Woman: Threesomes and the Erosion of the One-Time Rule of Homosexuality." *Sexualities*.

Sedgwick, Eve Kosofsky. 1985. *Between Men: English Literature and Male Homosocial Desire*. New York: Columbia University Press.

See, Sam. 2004. "Other Kitchen Sinks, Other Drawing Rooms: Radical Designs for Living in Pre-1968 British Drama." *Journal of Bisexuality* 4(3–4): 29–54.

Segal, Lynne. 1994. *Straight Sex: Rethinking the Politics of Pleasure*. Berkeley: University of California Press.

Seidman, Steven. 1993. "Identity and Politics in a 'Postmodern' Gay Culture: Some Historical and Conceptual Notes." In Michael Warner (Ed.), *Fear of a Queer Planet: Queer Politics and Social Theory*. Minneapolis: University of Minnesota Press.

Shannon, Deric, and Abbey Willis. 2010. "Theoretical Polyamory: Some Thoughts on Loving, Thinking, and Queering Anarchism." *Sexualities* 13(4): 433–443.

Sheff, Elisabeth. 2005. "Polyamorous Women, Sexual Subjectivity and Power." *Journal of Contemporary Ethnography* 34(3): 251–283.

Sheff, Elisabeth. 2006. "Poly-Hegemonic Masculinities." *Sexualities* 9(5): 621–642.

Sheff, Elisabeth. 2010. "Strategies in Polyamorous Parenting." In Meg Barker and Darren Langdridge (Eds.), *Understanding Non-Monogamies*. New York: Routledge.

Sheff, Elisabeth. 2011. "Polyamorous Families, Same-Sex Marriage, and the Slippery Slope." *Journal of Contemporary Ethnography* 40(5): 487–520.

Sheff, Elisabeth. 2013. *The Polyamorist Next Door: Inside Multiple-Partner Relationships and Families*. New York: Rowman & Littlefield.

Sommerville, Siobhan B. 2000. *Queering the Color Line: Race and the Invention of Homosexuality in American Culture*. Durham, NC: Duke University Press.

Starkweather, Katherine E., and Raymond Hames. 2012. "A Survey of Non-Classical Polyandry." *Human Nature* 23(1): 49–172.

Steinman, Erich. 2011. "Revisiting the Invisibility of (Male) Bisexuality: Grounding (Queer) Theory, Centering Bisexual Absences and Examining Masculinities." *Journal of Bisexuality* 11(4): 399–411.

Steward, Julian H. 1936. "Shoshoni Polyandry." *American Anthropologist* 38(4): 561–564.

Stockton, Kathryn Bond. 2007. *Beautiful Bottom, Beautiful Shame: Where "Black" Meets "Queer."* Durham, NC: Duke University Press.

Strauss, Gregg. 2012. "Is Polygamy Inherently Unequal?" *Ethics* 122(3): 516–544.

Symons, Donald. 1979. *The Evolution of Human Sexuality*. New York: Oxford University Press.

Taormino, Tristan. 2008. *Opening Up: A Guide to Creating and Sustaining Open Relationships*. San Francisco: Cleis Press.

Tolman, Debra. 2002. *Dilemmas of Desire: Teenage Girls Talk about Sexuality*. Cambridge, MA: Harvard University Press.

Touré. 2012. "Coming Out in Hip Hop: Frank Ocean's Powerful Moment." *Time*, July 5. http://ideas.time.com/2012/07/05/anderson-cooper-and-frank-ocean-a-tale-of-two-comings-out/#ixzz1zrWYsTj8.

Vassi, Marco. 2005. "Beyond Bisexuality." *Journal of Bisexuality* 5(2–3): 283–290.

Vassi, Marco. 2006. "Sex beyond Bisexuality." In R. Jackson (Ed.), *Bi Guys: The Deliciousness of His Sex*. Maple Shade, NJ: Lethe Press.

Veaux, Franklin, and Eve Rickert. 2014. *More than Two: A Practical Guide to Polyamory*. Portland, OR: Thorntree Press.

Vidal-Ortiz, Salvador. 2008. "'The Puerto Rican Way Is More Tolerant': Constructions and Uses of 'Homophobia' among Santeria Practitioners across Ethno-Racial and National Identification." *Sexualities* 11(4): 476–495.

Wagner, Brooke. 2009. "Becoming a Sexual Being: Overcoming Constraints on Female Sexuality." *Sexualities* 12(3): 289–311.

Waldby, Catherine. 1996. "Destruction: Boundary Erotics and Refigurations of the Heterosexual Male Body." In Elizabeth Grosz and Elspeth Probyn (Eds.), *Sexy Bodies: The Strange Carnalities of Feminism*. New York: Routledge.

Ward, Jane. 2008. "Dude Sex: White Masculinities and 'Authentic' Heterosexuality among Dudes Who Have Sex with Dudes." *Sexualities* 11(4): 414–434.

Ward, Jane. 2015. *Not Gay: Sex between Straight White Men*. New York: New York University Press.

Warner, Michael. 1999. *The Trouble with Normal: Sex, Politics, and the Ethics of Queer Life*. Boston: Harvard University Press.

Weinberg, Martin, Colin J. Williams, and Douglas Pryor. 1994. *Dual Attraction: Understanding Bisexuality* New York: Oxford University Press.

Wiederman, M. W. 1997. "Extramarital Sex: Prevalence and Correlates in a National Survey." *Journal of Sex Research* 34(2): 167–174.

Westermarck, Edward. 1926. *A Short History of Marriage*. New York: Macmillan.

Wilkinson, Eleanor. 2010. "What's Queer about Non-Monogamy Now?" In Meg Barker and Darren Langdridge (Eds.), *Understanding Non-Monogamies*. New York: Routledge.

Willey, Angela. 2006. "'Christian Nations,' 'Polygamic Races' and Women's Rights: Toward a Genealogy of Non/Monogamy and Whiteness." *Sexualities* 9(5): 530–546.

Williams, H. Sharif. 2010. "Bodeme in Harlem: An African Diasporic Autoethnography." *Journal of Bisexuality* 10(1–2): 64–78.

Worth, Heather, Alison Reid, and Karen McMillan. 2002. "Somewhere over the Rainbow: Love, Trust, and Monogamy in Gay Relationships." *Journal of Sociology* 38(3): 237–253.

Zanin, Andrea. 2013. "The Problem with Polynormativity." *Sex Geek: Thoughts on Sex and Life* (blog), January 24. https://sexgeek.wordpress.com/2013/01/24/theproblemwithpolynormativity/.

INDEX

Ahmed, Sara, 2–3, 62, 150
anal penetration, 155–157, 159; as prostage, 160
Anderson, Eric, 150
Another Country (Baldwin), 171
anti-racist desire, 171–172
Anzaldúa, Gloria, 29

Balasubramanian, Janani, 22
Baldwin, James, 171
Banderas, Antonio, 121
Barker, Meg, 16,
"Bend Over Boyfriend" pornography, 162
biphobia, 132, 74, 81, 142
bisexuality, 26–27, 69, 71, 81, 86, 94, 97, 103, 104, 140, 149, 152, 156, 159
bisexual pornography, 150
Back & Poly (Meetup group), 23
Black Girl Dangerous (website), 22
Block, Jenny, 47
Bond Stockton, Kathryn, 113
Boslo, Agnes, 163
Bourdieu, Pierre, 144
Boykin, Keith, 75
Branfman, Jonathan, 160
Brim, Matt, 171–172
Brown, Rodney McGruder, 72

Cardosa, Daniel, 63
Castle, Terry, 26,
charmed circle, 7, 146
cheating, 42–47, 51, 118–119; gender stereotypes, 43–47; narratives of, 33, 44–46
class, 67–68; habitus, 144
Clum, John, 132

compersion, 16–17
compulsory heterosexuality, 177n1
compulsory monogamy, 4–5, 13, 51, 58, 106–108, 120; effects, 13–14
Connell, R. W., 38,
consensual non-monogamy, 6, 12; erasure of, 13–14; research on, 12–13; utopian communities, 12
Coward, Noël, 132
critical race theory, 9–10
cross-racial touch, 165–167
cuckolding lifestyle, 149

Dean, Terrance, 72
Design for Living (Coward), 132–133
"devil's threesome," 149, 182n2
"down low," 33, 99; black respectability, 72, 88; definition, 73; and mononormativity, 80, 106–108; racism, 75; research, 80–82; stereotypes, 73–75; subculture, 86–87

erotic destruction, 153
erotic habitus, 144–145, 155; as mutable, 158–159; heterofeminine, 149, 152; heteromasculine, 149, 150, 152; gender differences, 145
evolutionary anthropology, 53–58; causes of gender differences, 53–54, 141, 154, 157

femininity, 38–38; embodiment, 153–156; erotic habitus, 145; politics of respectability, 100; polyqueer, 62–63; as possession, 47, 60; and sexual objectification, 46–47, 60–61, 115–116, 127, 157; sexual subjectivity, 60–63, 117, 125, 129, 133, 156

ABOUT THE AUTHOR

Mimi Schippers is Associate Professor of Sociology and Gender and Sexuality Studies at Tulane University. She is the author of *Rockin' Out of the Box: Gender Maneuvering in Alternative Hard Rock*.